"A great book with insightful stories about how marketing managers develop romantic, deep, and personal relationships between the brand and the consumer."

—Jagdish N. Sheth, Charles H. Kellstadt Professor of Marketing, Goizueta Business School, Emory University

"*Romancing the Brand* shows that a brand's strength, and ultimately its ability to generate significant talk value, lies in creating a meaningful consumer experience. People talk about—and advocate for—brands with which they have an emotional bond. Aided by entertaining stories about brands that have created 'love affairs' with the consumer, *Romancing the Brand* is an essential guide for marketers who are looking to strengthen their consumer relationships."

—Ed Keller, CEO, the Keller Fay Group, and coauthor, *The Face-to-Face Book* and *The Influentials*

"Emotional, educational, and effective, *Romancing the Brand* captures the timeless fundamentals of marketing, using contemporary examples and a framework one can relate to in a primal way. Tim Halloran shares insights that up-and-coming marketers, as well as global executives at the top of their game, will find valuable."

—Dick Patton, global chief marketing officer practice leader, Egon Zehnder

ROMANCING
THE
BRAND

HOW BRANDS CREATE
STRONG, INTIMATE RELATIONSHIPS
WITH CONSUMERS

TIM HALLORAN

JB JOSSEY-BASS™
A Wiley Brand

Cover design by Adrian Morgan
Cover image © Shutterstock

Published by Jossey-Bass
A Wiley Brand
One Montgomery Street, Suite 1200, San Francisco, CA 94104-4594—www
.josseybass.com

Jossey-Bass books and products are available through most bookstores. To contact
Jossey-Bass directly call our Customer Care Department within the U.S. at
800-956-7739, outside the U.S. at 317-572-3986, or fax 317-572-4002.

Wiley publishes in a variety of print and electronic formats and by print-on-
demand. Some material included with standard print versions of this book may not
be included in e-books or in print-on-demand. If this book refers to media such as
a CD or DVD that is not included in the version you purchased, you may
download this material at http://booksupport.wiley.com. For more information
about Wiley products, visit www.wiley.com.

Cataloging-in-Publication data on file with the Library of Congress.
978-1-118-61128-9 (cloth); 978-1-118-82896-0 (ebk); 978-1-118-82897-7 (ebk)

Printed in the United States of America
FIRST EDITION

HB Printing   10 9 8 7 6 5 4 3 2 1

CONTENTS

To Nancy, the romance of my life
and to
Henry, Jane, and Lydia

ROMANCING
THE
BRAND

1

ROMANCE AND THE BRAND

I had already been in the dark room for three-and-a-half hours, a bowl of peanut M&Ms in front of me, observing groups of women through a two-way mirror that felt like something out of CSI, as they explained their beverage consumption habits. Observing focus groups was a common practice for Coca-Cola brand managers. We were always striving to understand our consumers better so that we might find a way to connect with them. Our ultimate goal was to give folks like the women in this room a reason to purchase our brand rather than the hundreds of other options available to them.

I found myself wondering how much of what I did every day—trying to meet the needs of a finicky consumer base with some creative new message or compelling product improvement—was pointless. Did consumers really *care* about these brands? Looking around the observation room, I saw six or seven colleagues in various stages of engagement: among others, the assistant brand manager taking copious notes that would ultimately summarize our findings to our senior management, the agency account rep trying to infer something brilliant from a consumer's comment, and the marketing research manager making sure the moderator on the other side of the glass was covering everything on our checklist. All of us waiting, observing, listening for *anything* we could use in developing next year's marketing campaign. We needed to understand these women's thoughts and feelings about our brands in order to do our jobs.

But then something happened that subtly but profoundly changed my perception of how we as marketers should think about brands and the role they play in our consumers' lives.

It wasn't a particularly dramatic moment. The eight women sat around the overflowing table of colored cans and bottles of soft drinks. They had just completed what we call a "sorting" exercise, in which participants arranged soft drink brands in groups based on some organizing principle that they were to develop themselves. I don't remember how they organized the forty-plus brands that day, but what happened next stuck with me. A petite woman in her late twenties, picked up one of the cans and said to the focus group moderator, "I drink eight of these a day. It is always with me, no matter what happens. It was there when my boss gave me my promotion last week. It was at my side two months ago when my cat died. It got me through it. I start and end my day with it. It's never lets me down. I can always count on it. To sum it up, it's my boyfriend . . . Diet Coke."

MY BEVERAGE, MY BOYFRIEND

A wave of laughter hit the room, so loud that I'm sure the respondents could hear us on the other side of the two-way mirror. I sat up. Did she really say that Diet Coke was her boyfriend? How could one think of a can of sugar water (actually aspartame water in this case) in boyfriend terms? Commitment, intimacy, dependability—she felt all of these, not about Diet Coke, but *from* it. She loved it as a constant companion, a support mechanism, a celebratory friend. This was preposterous, wasn't it? We can't connect with products the same way we connect with people!

But in some important ways, that is just what we do. Academic studies have proven it repeatedly.[1] We don't just consume or interact with brands. We actually engage in relationships with them. With some brands, we have wild, short-term flings. Others stay with us for a lifetime, like family. Some brands offer us strictly utilitarian relationships—they are in our daily lives, yet we have no emotional connection to them. Maybe the brand feels like good medicine, like a physician, or maybe it's a loose connection, like a distant uncle you rarely see. Or maybe you rely on it, like a teacher, a coach, or even a parent. Each product and each consumer—and each relationship between the two—is different. But the young woman who so eloquently expressed her feelings about Diet Coke crystallized for me the simple truth that consumers engage in relationships with brands. If marketers were going to succeed, we would have to go beyond thinking about consumers as "target markets" that we needed to make aware of our brand and convince to purchase it. We needed to think about engaging consumers in a long-term relationship.

Think about it from your perspective as a consumer. Is there a brand that means something, *really means something* to you? Maybe there is a certain brand of clothing that you seek out first in a store. What about a certain brand of shoes that you must have? Perhaps you are willing to drive an extra two miles down the road past your local grocery store to Trader Joe's. Maybe when you order a Coke and the waiter asks whether Pepsi is OK, you say that it's not. Maybe when planning a business trip, you invariably check to see if your preferred hotel has a location in the city you are visiting. Think back to your childhood. Was there a video game system or doll that you absolutely had to have? When you were a teenager, was there a band whose new album you waited for with anticipation, snatching it up the day it was released?

All of these are examples of brands—products, retailers, or even people that make up the fabric of your everyday life. Sure they provide you with some recognizable functional benefits— the look and feel of a Polo shirt, the variety of organic lines at Whole Foods, or the entertainment value of the latest Maroon 5 song, but they also provide you much more. Maybe you feel that a brand says something about you to others when you are consuming, wearing, or using it. Or maybe you feel that the brand has a personality that you can relate to. Perhaps a brand occupies not only a specific place in your mind but also a specific place in your heart.

Now think about the first time you encountered that brand. Do you have a distinct memory of it? Was it "love at first sight," or did it take a while for you to adopt it? Has your relationship with that brand grown over time? Is it as strong today as it has ever been, or did it reach its peak some time ago and has now plateaued or even declined? Now imagine if that brand suddenly disappeared. How do things change? How do you feel? Can something easily replace it, or does its loss leave a hole in your life? Chances are that there are certain brands with which you've developed such a strong connection and with which you have engaged so frequently that if something were to happen, such as if they were discontinued or changed, you would feel a sense of loss—or even betrayal.

Having feelings toward brands seems to be a natural, powerful extension of how we're built as human beings. What does that mean to us as marketers? If we understand this, what do we do about it? Does it make sense for us to keep thinking about consumers as targets and demographic segments? Probably not. I'm convinced that this kind of thinking will only get us so far. I've come to believe that if marketers are going to succeed, we need to think about engaging consumers in a relationship—which, by definition, goes both ways. It has to be reciprocal. When a relationship is good, both parties get what they need the most and give their very best. The ideal brand-consumer relationship is one that is entered into by choice (because consumers *always* have a choice), that is both thrilling and dependable, and that is also based on trust: a romance.

Many brands—think Harley-Davidson, Apple, or Disney— have successfully created and cultivated a deep emotional connection with their consumer base. But how have they done it? And why does it matter today more than ever? Technology has given us a plethora of new tools that we don't fully understand or know how to use—primarily because we are trying to apply them within the context of an outdated way of thinking. If we don't think about marketing our brands in a completely different way—a way that is fundamentally based in the brand's relationship with the consumer—then we will never succeed.

My goal in this book is to get you thinking about how to connect with the consumer by creating and nurturing a genuine relationship—one that's as exciting and enduring as a great romance.

NEW PERSPECTIVES AND NEW PROBLEMS

At one point in time, marketers thought of brands as comprising attributes that encompass everything tangible about a product—its taste, packaging, ingredients, materials, logo, and so on. We sought to present these attributes in a way that met the needs of a certain identified consumer target group. In the language of classical marketing, the product's attributes together were supposed to "ladder up" to "functional benefits" that would help ease a consumer "pain point" or "need." For example, everything about a pair of Nike running shoes, from the width to the cushioning to the waffle sole, would be designed to meet a particular consumer's need for running shoes.

To do this, Nike might take a group of consumers—marathon runners, say—and divide that group into segments, all of whom had different needs when running, and demanded different features. There were high-arched marathon runners and low-arched marathon runners. There were marathon runners with wide feet and those with narrow feet. There were runners whose feet turned in and others whose turned out. Nike would develop different shoes that functionally met the specific needs of each identified runner segment. The thinking was that consumers would choose a product based on how well its attributes met their needs, looking also at more intangible elements—such as brand familiarity, perceived quality, and perceived value—and evaluating these in light of the product's price. For many brands and many categories, companies and consumers alike perceived this as a strictly cost-benefit association. A consumer mind-set might be, "Provide me these benefits, and I may pay more for your brand than for other options."

But marketers of some brands, especially those in categories where consumer passion was particularly strong, increasingly developed and marketed key benefits that tied into a consumer's *emotional* need state. The principle was that consumers felt so strongly about these brands that they would insist on using them, and if they couldn't, they would feel deprived emotionally. Nike is again a good example: to an avid runner, her shoes are essential in her quest to run well, run efficiently, and ultimately achieve goals that she has set for herself. Nike's functionality—its design, its comfort level, its cushioning—feeds these more personal needs, and the consumer becomes engaged emotionally. With its game-changing "Just Do It" campaign—its imagery of athletes achieving goals, winning, and succeeding—Nike accented the emotional side of its value proposition. The campaign helped make that marathon runner more confident that she would triumph—partly because she was wearing Nike.

Although "Just Do It" famously tapped into the importance that a consumer can place on a brand—both emotionally and functionally—there were as yet few theories in academia and little practice in industry that linked this type of brand-consumer connection to a relationship model. Marketing people mostly still gave higher priority to the functional and transactional nature of the brand-consumer interaction and still thought of it in a short-term context. Brands had target consumers, and marketing teams would develop annual plans to source volume from those consumers. Understanding the longer-term value behind emotionally connected consumer interactions wasn't a priority.

Then, in the mid-1990s, two doctoral students in marketing, one on either side of the country, began putting together separate but compatible theories that (1) brands had distinguishable, identifiable personalities, and (2) every brand and every consumer did in fact engage in a relationship similar to human relationships. Together these two theories supported a powerful new way of understanding how consumers interact with brands on a personal level.

The daughter of prominent marketing thinker David Aaker, Jennifer Aaker had marketing in her blood. As a young Stanford graduate student getting a joint PhD in marketing and psychology, she brought together both disciplines to create an intriguing theory that would map the dimensions of human personality onto brands. She used the theory to create a framework for determining the ways that brands were personified by consumers. After having more than six hundred consumers free-associate about one hundred personality attributes across a range of brands, Aaker found that consumers' perceptions of brand personalities closely mirrored their perception of human personalities. In other words, as consumers, we can be attracted to a brand not just by what it does for us functionally (following the conventional wisdom about why consumers chose products and brands), but by how well our personality fits what we perceive to be the brand's personality. In a way not unlike how we respond to other human beings, we might even be attracted to brands whose personalities we might not have, but might secretly desire (the classic "opposites attract" phenomenon).[2]

Meanwhile, Susan Fournier, an ex–Young and Rubicam advertising vice president who was now pursuing a PhD in marketing at the University of Florida, proposed a theory that would give insight into the relationships of brands and consumers. To develop her thesis, she went deep into the lives and brand choices of three women who represented different life stages, locations, and backgrounds.[3] She spent a significant amount of time with them, following their every move and experiencing their lives as they experienced them. In the time that she spent with these consumers, she found that brands were an inextricable part of their lives and saw that a mutual dependency existed in which the brand's stories and the individuals' life stories linked together.[4] From this understanding, she began to define a number of different relationships between consumers and brands. Relationships could range from competitive/hostile (your relationship with your cable company) to cooperative/friendly (maybe your relationship with your tennis racket) and from superficial/weak (perhaps your relationship with your dishwashing soap) to intense/strong (possibly your relationship with your toothpaste).[5] In short, the range of brand-consumer relationships was eerily similar to the range of human relationships. She concluded that the strongest brand-consumer relationships exhibited qualities comparable to those of happily married couples.

The work of these two researchers (as well as a plethora of additional marketing and psychological studies that have since been conducted on the topic) demonstrates that brand-consumer relationships do exist, are genuine, and have the ability to connect people to brands in unexpectedly deep and emotional ways.[6] This leads again to the bigger question that this book asks: What should we marketers do about it?

Meanwhile, beyond the halls of academia, marketing practice was evolving. Instead of just communicating product attributes and functional benefits, marketers across multiple product categories began to place a heavier emphasis on the emotional appeal in their messaging. Marketers of fashion, fragrances, soft drinks, beer, and athletic brands (to name a few) were starting to discover that making an emotional connection with a consumer was yet another way to differentiate their brands from the competition in crowded categories. Communications began focusing on brand "extrinsics" (the brand's personality and emotional qualities) rather than product "intrinsics" (the product's functional attributes and associated benefits), with the ultimate goal of connecting with consumers at a deeper level.

Although consumer communications still primarily used an interruption model, where most of the "talking" was from brand to consumer via one-way communications (that is, advertising) that consumers passively received, changes in that model were also beginning to occur. More emphasis was put on providing a unique, engaging experience by having brands figuratively "come to life." Think about brand activation at sporting events. At baseball stadiums, the reliance on static signs in the outfield was replaced by branding elements woven into the event. Take Turner Field in Atlanta, for example: every time the hometown Braves hit a home run, a forty-nine-foot-tall Coca-Cola bottle shot fireworks,[7] and, more recently, a forty-foot-tall Chick-fil-A Cow does the team's signature tomahawk chop.

Sampling programs were evolving too. Instead of just handing out product samples or coupons outside a store, brands would develop a traveling "show" in which samples were provided in the *context* of bringing the brand to life by entertaining consumers. For example, LEGO would invest and employ multiple "play" trucks that would tour the United States, stopping off in towns and creating big events where kids would spend *hours* interacting with the brand. Sure, brand representatives would hand out a coupon to every kid or give him or her a small sample LEGO set, but more important, they were interacting with the kids in an experiential environment that basically humanized the LEGO brand. Brands across the spectrum of categories were engaging in similar activities, seeking to become more holistically integrated into consumer lives.

Of course, as marketing evolved, it also received its share of criticism. Some marketing tactics, such as the glamorization of brands through sexual innuendo, puffery that bordered on dishonesty, and the use of exaggerated or blatantly dishonest claims, created an environment of distrust and distaste. As a result, consumers became increasingly cynical and distrustful of marketers, much of it the consequence of marketers' own actions.

Fast-forward to today. With the emergence of technology, social media, apps, and data analytics that tell us more about consumers than ever seemed possible, our means of engaging consumers have evolved yet again. Marketing has progressed to a model in which the consumer and brand now engage in a two-way dialogue. The continued advances in the technological space have created an environment where brands have the ability to communicate to consumers not just through a product experience or within the confines of a thirty-second television spot but in an ongoing, interactive manner, allowing consumers to communicate their preferences, desires, and needs directly back to the brand itself. There is a brave new world of opportunity for marketers to act as surrogates for their brands in their relationships with consumers.

We marketers have been quick to employ the new tools in our tool box, with some regrettable and even damaging results. On an almost daily basis, we hear another story about how marketers are taking advantage of consumers—making them (and their kids!) obese and unhealthy, invading their privacy with Big Brother–like tactics, and trying to manipulate them with fake claims and faulty science.

- In September 2011, Martin Lindstrom, the best-selling author of *Buyology*, publishes *Brandwashed: Tricks Companies Use to Manipulate Our Minds and Persuade Us to Buy*, "a shocking insider's look at how today's global giants conspire to obscure the truth and manipulate our minds, all in service of persuading us to buy" that promises, among other things, to reveal how advertisers and marketers intentionally target children when they are still in the womb and how they stoke the flames of public panic and capitalize on paranoia over global contagions, extreme weather events, and food contamination scares.[8]

- The *New York Times Magazine* publishes staff writer Charles Duhigg's "How Companies Learn Your Secrets," in which he relates a story about how Target, deploying the skills of its robust predictive analytics department (which is able to determine with staggering accuracy whether a woman is pregnant, based on what she purchases), sends a high school teenager a flyer and coupons congratulating her on her pregnancy—much to the surprise of her parents.[9]

- In October 2012, a *Huffington Post* article reports on a new marketing program from Verizon called Precision Market Insights, which collects data from smartphones and shares that information with potential advertisers. Bill Diggins, U.S. leader for the program, explains, "We're able to view just about everything they do." Colson Hillier, VP of the initiative, adds, "We realized we had a latent asset. We have information about how customers are using their mobile phones."[10]

The fact of the matter is that when some of us don't use our new tools, analytics, and technology in ways that are beneficial to our consumers, the whole profession suffers the consequences. Consumers are more cynical and less trusting than ever. And we marketers, who are tasked with building our company's or our client's brands, must seriously question whether we are in fact engaged in a worthy profession. We wonder whether every marketing activity will be judged as merely a feeble attempt to get a consumer to spend an extra dollar on our brand rather than a competitor's. Have we become the equivalent of snake oil salesmen—making false promises and setting expectations so high that our cynical society rejects our attempts to connect with consumers?

A NEW PARADIGM

When asked about how marketing differs today, Marc Mathieu, senior vice president of marketing at Unilever, said, "In the last few decades of the 20th century, marketing has become selling for the sake of selling, but at its inception, marketing was inspired by the Henry Fords, the William Levers of the world—people with a vision to bring products to people that could create progress and improve lives."[11] He's right. I believe that the way to get ourselves back on the right track is to build on the ideas formulated by Aaker and Fournier: to think about consumers as we would think about people we know well and care for deeply, and treat them accordingly.

The secret of successful marketing in this new age—the essential evolutionary next step—lies in creating and nurturing a powerful, passionate, and genuine relationship between the brand and consumer. The strongest brands have always viewed their consumer base in a relational manner—not as an entity to be taken advantage of but as a partner to engage, delight, and excite. Creating and managing strong relationships will be marketers' best answer to our critics, and our best shot at reviving the integrity of our profession. More important, this new approach will help a cynical consumer base start trusting us again. It's a paradigm shift that can bring new power, purpose, and effectiveness to a marketer's work.

Although Fournier shows that the brand-consumer relationship can take many forms, in this book I'll use the romantic relationship as a lens. I believe that it models the ideal brand-consumer relationship in key ways: it's a relationship of choice; it's deep and passionate; it's committed; and, at its best, it thrives on mutuality, trust, and respect—as well as excitement and delight. It takes time and effort to build, but it brings unmatched rewards. If we connect with our consumers and develop brand love, we will have achieved the ultimate brand-consumer relationship.

ROMANCING THE BRAND

Interdependence, energy, attention, commitment, mutual benefit. Successful relationships require all of these. As marketers, we are surrogates enabling a relationship between our brands and our customers to be manifested. This is how we provide value to both our customers and our brands. The most successful brands not only have strong, intimate relationships with their consumers but also work diligently to cultivate, manage, and grow those relationships in significant ways. Throughout *Romancing the Brand*, I will show you the principles that successful brands use to establish and grow the brand-consumer relationship, and the tools successful marketers use to connect consumers to brands in ways that go beyond a product's functional benefits.

These principles are

- Understand your consumers and their specialness
- Determine how you'll be different

- Tell your story and create an experience
- Have a compelling personality that shines through all your interactions
- Make your partner feel special
- Leverage your evangelists to spread the word
- Be honest
- Leverage mistakes and missteps to get stronger
- Make the relationship the highest priority in everything you do

Because I'm using romance as a lens for the brand-consumer relationship, the book's chapters echo stages of a maturing romantic relationship. Of course, a particular consumer may be in any of these relationship stages with a particular brand, but this approach does give us a road map as we consider how brands and consumers interact and evolve over their life spans. The chapters are

Know Yourself. The relationship starts with the brand. If you don't know who you are as a brand, how do you know which consumer will make a good relationship partner? In this chapter, we'll explore classical marketing practices for defining a brand's product benefits to set up the more intimate, emotional bonds.

Know Your Type. Every brand has an ideal consumer—someone who, when she connects with the brand, feels that that brand was made for her. The trick for marketers is to identify that ideal consumer, her functional, emotional, and social needs, and to perfect the match between those needs and what your brand offers. I'll introduce the type of consumer who ultimately determines whether the brand will succeed or fail.

Meet Memorably. The first few meetings between brand and consumer dictate whether the relationship has potential or whether it will remain in the mere acquaintance phase. In this chapter, we'll discuss establishing connections that are so special and memorable that a consumer desires to keep coming back for more.

Make It Mutual. Our strongest consumers should be influencers of others and, ultimately, brand evangelists. We'll discuss how, by understanding the proper role of classic and contemporary communication tools, we can leverage our connection with our strongest consumers so that they can spread our message to others.

Deepen the Connection. We'll discuss fostering the deeper bond with the consumer so that he experiences the brand as "a brand made for me," and look at ways to measure whether our romance with the consumer is still on track.

Keep Love Alive. As the brand-consumer relationship matures, rejuvenating the relationship through innovation and news is essential. In this chapter, we'll discuss ways to stay in touch (or get back in touch) with consumer needs.

Making Up. Just as in our own relationships, brands and consumers go through crises. How this is managed will determine whether a relationship is strengthened or devalued.

Breaking Up and Moving On. Relationships end. Either we recalibrate and start engaging with a new consumer group or we fail forward, eliminate the brand, and, using what we've learned, develop stronger consumer relationships with different products.

To bring these principles to life, I'll share stories about best-in-class consumer-brand relationships so that you can see for yourself the power of the romance paradigm in action. You'll learn what works and what doesn't in cultivating the brand-consumer relationship by hearing directly from the marketers who don't just manage some of the world's largest and best-known brands but actively work to build and grow relationships with consumers on a daily basis and have achieved outstanding results in the process.

- Matt Kahn will showcase how a small local bottled water established such a strong reputation that it went from being sold out of the back of a car to being the top premium bottled water in the country in just a few years.
- Kersten Rivas, Katy Milmoe, Willem Jan van der Hoeven, and Paul Smailes will share how the "Most Interesting Man in the World" created a national movement behind the Dos Equis brand.
- Stuart Sheldon will talk about the power of the brand experience and how it blows away any social media campaign in terms of spreading word of mouth.
- Jeff Gregor will demonstrate how a brand that one might wrongly perceive as being for your grandparents is so strong that fans tattoo the logo on their skin.

- Christy Amador will share insight into the power of brand innovation and examples of bringing new dimensions to a brand-consumer relationship that is over 120 years old.
- Blake Hawley and Cigdem Topalli will show how a brand that was once a laughingstock can be turned around.
- Jim Smith will discuss how the Atlanta Falcons brand went from absolute disaster in the wake of the Michael Vick dogfighting scandal to starting over and recreating a stronger relationship with its consumer base.
- Darryl Cobbin will show how a brand that once focused on moms became the number-one teen brand in the country.
- Steve Hutcherson will discuss what was deemed by many to be the biggest flop in marketing history—and what happened then.

The overriding message of this book is that establishing a relationship with consumers is a game changer for marketers, and my goal here is simple. If you are a marketer, this book will help you identify the right consumer with whom to engage in a relationship, "meet" that consumer in the right context, evolve and strengthen the relationship, and, on occasion, decide when to start over or move on.

Marketing is changing. Consumers are changing. The way both interact with each other is always changing. Brands that have been and will be successful will be the ones that cultivate and grow relationships with consumers that reach them at the physical, emotional, and, dare I say, soulful level. Those brands that can't interact with consumers in this way risk failure. Those that can will succeed. Let's see how it is done.

2

KNOW YOURSELF

How often have you heard that before you can understand others, you have to understand yourself? In other words, to really know what we want in a relationship, we have to know ourselves. We have to understand what is special about us, what we bring to the table in a potential courtship, and, let's face it, what we do better than others who may be courting the same individual. Now, when we put ourselves out there on the dating scene, we probably don't go through a laundry list of what our strengths are, where our interests lie, and why we would make a good partner to another individual. But if you think about your relationships, you'll see that even on a subconscious basis, you definitely have an understanding of what you are all about, what you like and don't like to do, and what that might mean in terms of a prospective mate. You aren't going to enjoy being with someone who has radically different goals, beliefs, or interests than you have. Not to discount the idea that "opposites attract," but even those couples have something that draws them together that they can share. It's all about finding something in common that attracts one to the other.

With brands and consumers, it is no different. As marketers, we play the role as surrogates for our brand. We are the ones who will ultimately make decisions about how the brand looks, acts, and behaves in the marketplace. We will ultimately decide on the type of consumers with whom we will want to engage in a relationship. We will reach out to them, engage with them, and, we hope, touch them in such a way that they choose our brand over other options.

For you to be successful, you must be able to understand what is special about your brand. This is especially true when you find yourself newly assigned to an existing brand or business. Unless you are dealing with a new product with essentially a clean slate, you inherit the brand, its history, its existing relationships, and its current dynamic within the category in which it competes. Only by thoroughly immersing yourself and uncovering the unique qualities present between brand and consumer will you be able to make your own impact on the brand-consumer relationship. What is truly unique about the product behind the brand? How different are you from other options? Expanding on that, where is an opening that may be ripe for opportunity? After all, if you don't completely and thoroughly understand your brand, how can you expect a consumer to? Once you know yourself, it makes it all that much easier to know your type—the desired consumer who will be your brand's best match.

Coming to know yourself (that is, to know your brand) requires that you

- *Determine how you'll be different.* To stick out in our crowded world, you must differentiate yourself from the other options that are also striving for your consumer's attention.
- *Discover that one thing.* Determining one thing that you can own, *really own*, in the heart and mind of your consumer will go a long way to breaking out from the crowd.
- *Dig deep.* Don't ever say you can't find something to own. Search high and low in terms of what your brand offers that is unique and better than others. It may come from the most unlikely of places.

In this chapter (and throughout the book), we'll look at each of these ideas, using stories of powerful brand-consumer relationships to illustrate the points in a real-world setting. As is true of many stories throughout the book, some of these cases will resurface in later chapters where they'll illustrate different points; others will focus on one particular lesson. Taken together, they all provide a road map to building and maintaining strong and lasting brand-consumer relationships.

Let's get started with a story close to home for me—a story about the first brand to which I was assigned.

DETERMINE HOW YOU'LL BE DIFFERENT

As the sun shone through the large window in the rotunda, it gave off an almost blinding light accentuated by the bright white marble walls of the grand entrance of The Coca-Cola Company. Standing in the lobby of a building that could have been mistaken for the Capitol or another edifice of equal stature, I was an anxious twenty-five-year-old assistant brand manager waiting for his new manager to take him to his office at the world's largest marketing company. Little did I know that I would be spending the next ten years on the brand management floor, seeking to develop brand relationships with various consumer groups.

In late 1994, after getting a master's in marketing research from the University of Georgia, I took a new job in the brand management group at The Coca-Cola Company. Coke was starting a new division called the Non Carbonated Beverages Group. It would be a laboratory for innovation and new products designed to focus on the growing health and wellness trend. Coke was late to the party—many of the categories in which we planned to compete were well entrenched with formidable competitors. Nevertheless, if the company was going to be a total beverage company, it would need to embrace this category.

So Coke was looking for brand managers who would be able to persevere on upstart brands that didn't have much chance of success. I was the assistant brand manager on the brand that probably had the hardest mountain to climb: Powerade. The sports drink category was dominated by Gatorade, which for all intents and purposes *was* the category. (Gatorade was developed at the University of Florida in the late 1960s to help keep Gator football players hydrated during steamy practices and games on their North Central Florida campus.) When a brand is as dominant and entrenched as Gatorade was (its share of the sports drink category was 88 percent), and it is twelve times bigger than the competing brand you're marketing, you have to ask yourself, "What consumer can we get to even consider engaging in a relation-ship with us? And how?"

In the case of Gatorade versus Powerade, there was little difference in the products themselves. Powerade was a "me-too" product with the same flavors, similar packaging, and even the same "ade" suffix. The only noticeable differ-ence, and it was a functional product difference rather than a meaningful brand advantage, was that Powerade's formula at the time contained a complex carbohydrate, maltodextrin, which enabled the brand to claim that it had a third more carbohydrates than Gatorade. For knowledgeable athletes, car-bohydrates equaled energy, but most consumers didn't make that connection.

So our goal was to discover a consumer group that might one day find Powerade more appealing than Gatorade, even though the products were so similar. At that time (and still), the bulk of sports drink consumption came from eighteen- to twenty-nine-year-old males. In fact, if you looked at every male of this age across the country, you would find that, on average, each one drank about one sports drink a week, with many of them drinking it on a daily basis. Mostly, they had been drinking Gatorade for anywhere from ten to twenty years. They enjoyed it. There wasn't a problem with it. How would we ever get them to switch to a brand whose only differentiating factor was that it offered "33% more carbohydrates"?

The short answer was, we wouldn't. We weren't going to get these guys to leave a romance to which they were already committed. They were loyal to Gatorade. It was working fine for them. Trying to change their behavior would cost considerable time and money and would ultimately result in failure. Think of it this way: which is easier, trying to start a relationship with someone who is single, available, and "looking" or with someone who has been in a committed relationship for years? So we made the deliberate decision to abandon the largest market segment—to ignore everyone over the age of eighteen, because no one over eighteen was looking to engage in a relationship with a different sports drink. The under-eighteen crowd, however, showed promise. According to our data,

- Ninety-nine percent of teens drank sports drinks, with 52 percent drinking one or more per week.
- Sports drinks were the favorite beverage of eight- to eleven-year-olds.
- Each successive five-year cohort of teens was drinking more sports drinks than the previous cohort.

Teens, we found, weren't just discovering sports drinks but *embracing* them. They were participating in organized sports earlier than previous generations, and because sports seemed to open the door to sports drink consumption, it made sense that sports drinks were becoming a bigger piece of teen beverage consumption. (In our research, half of teens indicated that their last consumption of a sports drink occurred during an athletic activity.) Furthermore, teens played a huge role in the choice of brands. Some 80 percent of sports drink purchase decisions were influenced by teens, with 58 percent actually purchasing the brand themselves. For those purchases where Mom was still playing an active role in the choice, sports drinks were seen by her as a healthier beverage alternative to soft drinks and juices due to their lower sugar content. All these facts gave us confidence that if we focused our efforts on romancing the next generation of sports drink users, we might succeed.

Isn't that what strategy is all about? It's about making an informed choice and following through on it. Our choice was determined by our thorough understanding of how consumers interacted with the category, our brand, and the competition. Gatorade didn't just own sport drink history, it owned the category. We knew we couldn't compete head-on with such a dominant brand, so we had to look for an opening—any opening—that might offer us the opportunity to engage in a relationship with one part of the sports drink category. Understanding our own brand and how it differed from the competition was the first step to ultimately getting there. This understanding started with the product itself.

Without a physical product or service, you have no brand. The brand brings a generic product alive in the consumer's mind. But underneath it all, you must have a compelling product offering. Guy Kawalski, who worked along Steve Jobs for years, once said, "What Steve did that few marketers under-stand is that he first created a great product. It's hard to market crap. Most marketers take whatever crap is thrown at them and put lipstick on the pig. Steve's 'secret' was to control the product *and* the marketing, not just the marketing."[1]

The specific attributes of the product that you are market-ing must be the starting point of any relationship that a brand is going to have with a consumer. These are the actual tangible aspects and physical characteristics of the product. In human terms, it's how the brand "looks." It is what makes you "check someone out." Being attracted to product attributes is a bit like being attracted to another person's physical features. Although attractive physical features will only get someone so far, they are often what makes us notice someone else. Similarly, understanding a brand's relevant and compelling product attributes is also a starting place.

So what do I mean by product attributes? A *product attribute* is anything that is physically part of the product. Flavors, packages, logos, processes, materials, traditions, and formulas all are considered product attributes. Product attributes tell us a lot about the product, but nothing about what the brand will do for the user. In the Powerade example, "33% more carbohydrates than Gatorade" is a product attribute, and it was the one we chose at first to use as the foundation of our first national campaign. However, "33% more carbohydrates than Gatorade" didn't initially connect with consumers until (as we'll see later) we were able to connect it to something bigger—a benefit that meant something to them.

Finding compelling product attributes will drive us to something that is important to the brand's relationship with the consumer—tangible benefits. *Tangible* or *functional benefits* can be defined as ways the brand actually fulfills a need of the user. When we talk about *needs* in the context of functional benefits, we are talking specifically about physical needs like curbing hunger, cushioning feet, making a call, getting from point A to point B, and so on. (There are other kinds of needs and associated benefits; we'll talk about those more in the next chapter.) Sometimes a brand can develop a functional benefit that is, by itself, so compelling and unique that it is enough to differentiate the brand from others seeking to have a relationship with a consumer. But most of the time the physical product attributes and their associated tangible benefits merely serve to create a foundation for a more complex and emotionally based consumer relationship. This was the route the Powerade team took. We'll be spending a lot of time discussing the emotional qualities of brand-consumer relationships, but for now, it is important to remember that good marketers start by uncovering those special product attributes that will in turn lead to meaningful functional benefits and will ultimately give the brand its best chance of forming an emotionally engaging consumer relationship.

• • •

When we're working with an existing brand in a well-established category, like sports drinks, product attributes are typically already developed and may have to be aligned with an existing consumer need. With a new product, the need may actually drive the product's key attribute—a product characteristic that is the basis of its brand appeal. This was the case with smartwater.

In 1993, a water contamination scare hit serial entrepreneur Darius Bikoff's Manhattan neighborhood. Little did anyone—even Bikoff—guess that this small crisis would spur the creation of the top-selling premium bottled water in the country. At the time of the scare, Bikoff had never bought bottled water before—after all, New York City's water was among the best-tasting and cleanest in the world. But when he couldn't drink tap water any longer, he found a sea of sameness in the bottled water aisle of the bodega at the bottom of his high rise. Brand after brand presented mountain streams and evocations of France or nature. He had no idea which water was better than the others—or if there *was* one better than the others.

Bikoff became intrigued with the possibility of competing in the category with his own product. He dove into research, joining trade groups and reading industry publications. As someone who cared about his health and what he was putting into his body, Bikoff was interested in developing a better, healthier water.[2]

One of the first things he discovered was that many existing bottled waters were sourced from streams and rivers. The imagery was nice—after all, aren't crisp, clean mountain streams about as pure and natural as you can get? But in reality, he learned, spring water collects contaminants in the ground— things he did not want to put in his body. Could he create a bottled water that didn't have those contaminants?

Bikoff essentially took himself back to fourth grade to study the hydrologic cycle—the continuous movement of water on, above, and below the surface of the Earth. It's how water is "made" in the natural environment. Bikoff's idea was that he would recreate vapor distillation—nature's way of purifying water—in a factory environment.

But an interesting point about pure H_2O is this: it doesn't taste that good. It tastes flat. So Bikoff's development team decided to add a combination of minerals, including potassium, magnesium, and calcium, to the water to round out its taste. So Bikoff's bottled water would have two relevant attributes—purity and mineral content—that led to two functional benefits—good taste and hydration. This was even reflected in the chosen brand name, smartwater, which was derived from the hydrologic cycle (*hydro* = water and *logic* = smart). More important, both the attributes and the functional benefits could be *laddered up* to the kinds of emotional benefits that we'll intensely focus on later, which make for a strong brand-consumer connection: the water was "smart," both in how it was developed and in how it would make consumers feel when they chose it. In 1996, the smartwater brand was born.

FIND THE ONE THING

Of course, just because you've determined how you'll be different, that by itself doesn't guarantee success. To be able to meet a tangible consumer need and discover those compelling attributes, you must act on one overarching principle. Not doing it will result in failure. It is a simple concept in theory—and a very familiar one—yet it is so difficult to actually execute that most marketers violate it. I am talking about exercising the discipline to focus on and own *just one thing*—just one core idea in the consumer's mind. You know this rule, and probably have for years, but have you been implementing it? Does every touchpoint with your consumer reflect that one idea you are trying to communicate?

For the most part, it is difficult for marketers to keep to one idea because they have so many great things to say about their brand. They believe, usually with good reason, that their brand has many strong benefits, such that limiting messaging to one core idea is close to impossible. Yes, most brands have lots of value associated with them, and lots of benefits. But it is as your romance with your consumer grows that all these wonderful things about your brand will emerge. The principle of the one thing speaks to your initial reputation. It's the characteristic that will make someone interested enough to want to find out more—to want to *meet*. Consumers are exposed to over three thousand messages a day, and for your brand to break through the clutter, you must identify and consistently communicate that one idea. So how do you find it?

Forgo

The first way to own one thing is to *forgo* any others. That's right. To own an idea in the consumer's mind, we have to give up *everything* else. For years, whenever I've asked a room full of people, whether they are students or executives, "Who makes safe cars?" one (and only one) brand is mentioned. In unison, the group shouts out "Volvo!" Why do you think that is? It is because Volvo has consistently and dogmatically preached safety at every consumer touchpoint. If you ask Volvo owners, they will tell you that Volvo has many lovable qualities beyond safety. They might talk about the ride, the handling, the comfort, or the style. Any of these things may be important qualities of Volvo and its consumer romance. But none of these is what Volvo talks about when it introduces itself. None of these is what Volvo's reputation is built upon. Volvo is *all* about safety. That simple message has been able to cut through the clutter and represent Volvo for *years*.

You can see the same phenomenon across categories. Strong brands give up potentially lucrative messages that diverge from their signature quality. Whole Foods gives up mainstream brands; Nike gives up dress shoes. In fact, when

Nike saw an opportunity to compete in the dress shoe category, it bought Cole Hahn, but it didn't change the Cole Hahn line to be branded as Nike. Why? Because that would violate what Nike was all about. Nike is about athletic shoes, not dress shoes.[3] There's no doubt that the practice of forgoing keeps strong brands from generating product lines, entering business ventures, and expanding brand messaging in ways that might represent nice short-term business propositions. However, if you do not forgo these, you risk blurring the brand's overall message and damaging its existing relationship. Strong brands don't give in to the temptation.

Win Something

The ability to be seen as a winner—as a brand that wins something at the expense of competitors—is another way to own one thing. Consumers remember and like winners. If you are perceived to be the winner of a specific benefit or category, you are going to be a leader in the marketplace and a brand that the consumer keeps in mind.

You might be thinking, "What if every benefit in my category has one clear winner? There is a brand that is seen as the leader in all the major ways my category is defined." I say, look again. Examine your category to look for unique ways that the category may be defined or redefined. For instance, smartwater wasn't the first bottled water. It wasn't the first premium water. But smartwater *was* the first bottled water to be developed the way that water is created in nature (through the hydrologic process). That was ownable. Even if another competitor tries to manufacture water in the same way, smartwater has been talking about it now for years. It owns it. If a competitive water company also starts talking about the process, what could it say? We use more of the hydrologic process? It just doesn't make sense: smartwater wins "the first water made via the hydrologic process." Other examples of the *win something* strategy include Grey Poupon, which was not the first mustard but the first gourmet mustard, and Starbucks, which was not the first coffee shop but the first branded coffee experience.

Think about what your brand can win. Here's a hint: even if you aren't the first to actually offer a particular attribute or benefit, if no one is talking about it, grab it! It's ripe for the taking. Remember, it's all about perception, and if you are perceived to be the winner, then you are the winner (even if someone got there before you). Of course, there might be a reason why no one has adopted that positioning. Immerse yourself in your brand's consumer and category to determine whether or not your "winning" proposition is compelling enough to cause consumers to want to meet you.

Look Within

The power of the smartwater positioning was that it started with the product itself. The natural hydrologic process combined with the electrolyte enhancement set the foundation for "smart" hydration. Every brand has the opportunity to leverage something about its internal DNA: how it's made, its history, its expertise, its ingredients, its people, its processes. These are all blank canvases for creating a compelling reputation. If something about a brand's DNA can be tied into a consumer need, it can become a powerful differentiator.

Consider the Budweiser "Born On" initiative, which is still an integral part of the brand today. It emerged from the brand's distribution system. Because of Budweiser's strong network of distributors, it has a very efficient route to market. That, by itself, may not be compelling. Who really cares that Budweiser has a lot of distributors and gets to stores quickly? However, research into the needs of beer drinkers indicated that stale or "skunky" beer is an underlying fear. Beer drinkers want to know that the beer they're drinking is "fresh." Budweiser's robust distribution system and consistently high consumer demand gives it a very fast sell-through rate in retail stores. It doesn't take much time for the brand to land in people's homes after it is produced. So Budweiser took an internal strength, fast production and distribution, and aligned it with a user desire, the avoidance of "skunky" beer, to create a compelling proposition: the "Born On" proposition, which states unequivocally that beer goes bad within 110 days and guarantees that Budweiser, because it is "brewed in twelve locations nationwide," will never be stale. As Budweiser's website puts it, "So, no matter where you are, we can get it to you faster, and more importantly, fresher." In fact, Budweiser has expanded this initiative through the power of technology: through a free Track Your Bud app, users can track the origins of the beer they're holding in their hand.

DIG DEEP

Finding unique, differentiating product attributes and functional benefits may not be easy. After all, smartwater was *developed* around a unique manufacturing process. Most brands don't have the luxury of starting from scratch. As a marketer, you have to work with what you have—challenging, but not impossible, and with diligence and persistence, the results can be fantastic.

What if, for example, a brand is in a category in which many of the product attributes and functional benefits are similar among competitors? What if the category comprises more than twenty thousand brands worldwide? This is what the team at Dos Equis encountered in 2007 as they took stock of their brand: a small Mexican beer that was bordering on obscurity.

Dos Equis was originally brewed by Cuauhtemoc-Moctezuma Brewery and was licensed to Heineken to market and distribute. There was little brand awareness or identity beyond Mexico, and the beer was distributed in just a few southwestern U.S. states. But during a routine brand analysis in 2007, the Dos Equis brand team started noticing something interesting. According to Willem Jan van der Hoeven, the Dos Equis brand director at the time, "We had noticed that Dos Equis, as a Mexican brand, had started making inroads in, of all places, Austin, Texas. We started to realize that University of Texas [UT] students were discovering the brand during their spring break in Mexico, and when they returned to Texas, one state where we had distribution, they were drinking it quite frequently."[4]

Van der Hoeven believed that Dos Equis might have untapped potential in the United States. Another Mexican beer, Corona, had become a major player in the U.S. beer category; could there be room for a second mass-marketed Mexican beer? After all, UT students had gone to Mexico, found this brand, and realized that it was available in Texas.

Van der Hoeven's hypothesis, confirmed by Austin sales, was that these students wanted to bring back a bit of the Mexican culture that they had experienced during spring break, found the brand available in Texas when they returned, and began to adopt it. Spring break is a college ritual that leaves an indelible mark on many students. If Dos Equis was becoming part of that experience—at least for the students who were spending spring break in Mexico—the brand might be positioned as a reminder of spring break. This was already starting to happen; van der Hoeven and his team, which included Havas World-wide Agency partners Kersten Rivas and Katy Milmoe, thought they might be able to accelerate a relationship with Dos Equis and these twenty-somethings.

They set out to understand what the existing reputation of Dos Equis was among both those who had experienced the brand in Mexico over spring break and those who had not. They did both formal and informal research, sometimes sitting down with consumers in bars, and found that most people, at least those who hadn't discovered it on spring break, had little association with Dos Equis. According to account director Milmoe, their perception of the brand was that it was "something akin to a beer that I get in Mexican restaurants when they don't have the brand I want."[5]

The brand they wanted was Corona. In their minds, Corona was undoubtedly Mexico. It owned both the country and the culture. In a classic positioning sense, Corona had "won" Mexico. As Milmoe said, "Corona had a feel. It was beaches, relaxation, vacations, and sun. But we thought to ourselves, is there anything else about Mexico that might link better to Dos Equis? As it turns out, there was."

In trying to understand the potential corridors in which to position the brand, the team first looked specifically at Dos Equis intrinsics, those attributes that were part of the product. One of those was the brand's history. Dos Equis was originally developed by a German brewmaster who had moved to Mexico and established a brewery. So, in actuality, it was a beer recipe brought over from Europe that just happened to be set in Mexico. It was first developed at the tail end of the 1890s and launched to celebrate the arrival of the twentieth century. In fact, that is how it got the name Dos Equis (Spanish for "two Xs," twenty in Roman numerals). Although considered a lighter lager, it had a heavier and more unique taste than typical U.S. light beers such as Coors Light or Bud Light. If anything, its German, turn-of-the-century beginning, combined with its Mexican setting, created something of a hybrid beer.

Among the few who were familiar with Dos Equis (those college spring breakers), many saw it quite differently from Corona. In those early conversations, when consumers were educated about the Dos Equis brand, the team found that the unique name, the imposing XX, the shiny gold label, the German brew master, and the slightly different taste created an air of mystery around the brand. The idea of *mystery* intrigued the team: it linked to a Mexico that many didn't immediately associate with beer. Adds Milmoe, "We did some exploration of what Mexico meant, and yes, the sun-and-fun Corona imagery was very strong. But there was something else about Mexico that started to fascinate us: the nighttime Mexico that was mysterious, unknown, and off the beaten path. Dos Equis represented *that* Mexico. We were more than beaches and burritos."

It was an intriguing starting point, but stopping there wouldn't yield much of a connection. What consumer need could the brand's product attributes, which included its mysterious origins, unique taste, and Mexican heritage, meet? How could these attributes be narrowed down to one core idea? More important, how could that core idea result in a compelling reason for a consumer to pick up a Dos Equis instead of one of the thousands of other beer choices available? The team had significantly more work to do. They would need to understand the consumer much more intimately. They would have to build on these insights, not just to develop a functional reason for a consumer to enter into a relationship with the brand, but to find an emotional connection that would lead the consumer to actively seek out Dos Equis. As we'll see in later chapters, the insights that they ultimately found, and the remarkable emotional connection that resulted, took this small, mostly unknown beer into the stratosphere.

TRANSITIONING TO EMOTIONALLY DRIVEN CONNECTIONS

In this chapter, we've talked a lot about the basics of identifying the underlying strengths of your brand's product. It is critical to understand what unique product attributes your brand possesses and how they might meet one of the needs of your consumers in a way that is different from the competition. This is half of the equation.

The other half of establishing a brand-consumer relationship—truly connecting with consumers—lies in really getting to know the consumers: their interests, attitudes, and beliefs.

What are they really looking for? Why are they even seeking out the category? What do they find attractive? The answers require some digging. If you go up to a random consumer and ask him why he likes a certain brand, you'll most likely hear a litany of functional reasons: Brand X tastes great, looks good, curbs my hunger, runs software faster, is safe, has more features, and so on. These are all compelling physical reasons. But they aren't emotional reasons. Make no mistake: the emotional reasons are there, whether or not the consumer articulates them or really even recognizes them. And they are often the more powerful reasons a consumer chooses a brand. Only when you dig deeper do you find them.

As marketers, we are always looking to differentiate our product from the competition. And here is a clue to the mystery of how a brand can establish a relationship with consumers: consumers can have only so many functional needs, and brands can have only so many functional benefits. Within a category, there are, by definition, a set amount of functional needs that can be met; otherwise the category would change, right? There are only so many functional reasons that a person will eat cereal, for example. It can curb her hunger, taste great, give her a healthy start to the day, give her necessary vitamins, and so on, but after a while, you will start running out of physical needs that cereal can meet. So if there are multiple brands within a category, you'll immediately start overlapping with competitors on meeting physical consumer needs. In fact, if competitors are all functionally oriented, a category will soon evolve into an attribute-oriented competition, with each brand trying to one-up the other by adding attributes. Once a competitor copies the benefit, the first brand is back to square one and must find yet another augmentation to differentiate itself. You can see where this ultimately (and rather quickly) leads: into a game of one-upmanship and a major resource drain.

In the next chapter, we will discuss how to ladder your product's attributes and associated functional benefit in a way that creates a more complex emotional consumer bond. *Laddering* is simply building on the strong foundation you've created with your product to develop more intimate connections. These emotional connections with the consumer are essential in building the romance.

For now, the important thing to remember is that behind every stated physical need lie higher-order emotional needs that must also be met. Although a grounding in the brand's physical features (that is, product attributes) is essential, that knowledge won't matter without an understanding of the emotional connection. Conversely, any attempt at an emotional connection is doomed without a strong functional proposition. Product attributes and functional benefits are the lead into the conversation with the consumer (remember the "one thing"), and they are also the steak behind the emotional sizzle. If the groundwork hasn't been laid, then a consumer base will lose faith and grow cynical, and any emotional connection to the brand that might have been created will be lost. For any romance—whether between brand and consumer or between two people—to last, you start with self-knowledge. With a sense of yourself, you're ready to meet and connect. That's what the next chapter is about.

3

KNOW YOUR TYPE

The grainy sepia-toned images seem out of place and mysterious. You feel as though you are watching footage from a foreign country or from someone's old home movie collection. On the screen is a young man with a full, dark beard coming out of the ocean carrying what looks like a treasure chest. People gather around him, excited, to see what he has brought in from the sea. A male voice, deep and rich, without the slightest trace of humor, says, "People hang on his every word, even the prepositions."

Cut to color footage of the same man, now much older, on top of a mountain unhooking a rope connecting a white grand piano to a helicopter. "He can disarm you with his looks or his hands . . . either way."

Cut to the man, now running at full speed and carrying a fox, while being chased by three men wearing red on horseback. "He can speak French . . . in Russian." Cut again to the man in a large study putting markers on a global map, only to be interrupted by an owl flying through the room and landing on his shoulder. "He is . . . the Most Interesting Man in the World."

Cut at last to an intimately lit bar, where our hero, now cleaned up and wearing a white button-down shirt and black blazer with red handkerchief, sits at a table with beautiful women at least forty years younger than he. He looks into the camera and softly says with a subtle Mexican accent, "I don't always drink beer, but when I do, I prefer Dos Equis."

We get a beauty shot of a bottle of Dos Equis, with its shiny gold label and red XX logo, and the Most Interesting Man in the World gives us one final message: "STAY THIRSTY, *my friends.*"

THE MOST INTERESTING MAN IN THE WORLD

The series of ads aptly titled "The Most Interesting Man in the World" sparked what Havas Worldwide managing director Kersten Rivas called "a cultural phenomenon." A century-old but little-known brand (heretofore familiar mostly to spring breakers) had come to the table with a communication the likes of which the American beer consumer had never seen. It was 180 degrees away from the slapstick, sophomoric hijinks that were the status quo for most beer commercials in 2010.

Within a few years, Dos Equis would become the sixth-largest imported beer, its "Most Interesting Man" campaign permeating popular culture to the extent that it was parodied on *Saturday Night Live*. With this communication, a beer brand whose relationship with even those consumers who had "met" it before had been casual at best, became the beer that everyone wanted to "date."

As we saw in the last chapter, the Dos Equis team had started by doing work to better "know themselves"—or more specifically to understand those product attributes and consumer benefits that were unique to the brand. They had discovered that the combination of Dos Equis' mysterious origins, unique taste, and Mexican heritage might be a key to its standing out in an incredibly crowded beer category. But how did they get from the brand's mysterious, Mexican product attributes to the Most Interesting Man in the World? For starters, they completely immersed themselves in the lives of their potential consumer, the twenty-something male beer drinker. (Yes, females drink beer, but their overall numbers pale significantly in comparison to those of males.) The team committed to learning more about "their type."

Getting to Know the Twenty-Something Beer Drinker

To learn about these guys, the Dos Equis team, led by global brand director Willem Jan van der Hoeven, didn't commission impersonal surveys or conduct focus groups in an artificial setting. Rather, the brand team and their colleagues, the Havas agency, went to where the beer drinker was—the bars. Their goal was to discover who this beer drinker was by experiencing life as he experienced it while engaging with the brand. As Havas managing director Kersten Rivas put it, "We had to dive deep into their mind-set. The research we did was guerrilla-type research. We engaged in conversations in bars. We got to know them in a personal way. We wanted to know how they engaged with their friends, specifically in the context of the bar scene."[1] So the team spent night upon night in various bars in multiple cities talking to the guys who they believed represented the biggest opportunity for the brand. What they found was revealing.

First, according to Rivas, many of the guys they talked to were dismissive of beer advertising. "They felt that the beer category spoke to them in a dumbed-down fashion. It was frat-boy-like humor." Many of them didn't want to be seen that way—as the butt of jokes. In fact, many actually feared being perceived the way that beer ads depicted them. For these guys, the last thing they wanted in a group setting was to be looked down on or condescended to. There is a big difference between getting your friends to laugh *with* you and having your friends laugh *at* you. Sharing your own sense of humor and your own opinions, thoughts, and beliefs also carried with it a big risk.

The team found that the crux of these young men's fear was to be thought of as *boring*. According to Rivas, "They shared this common fear—that I'm not substantial enough, I don't have enough good stories to tell." Milmoe added, "When they went out, they ultimately would want to be a part of conversations in which they could talk about their skydiving adventures and hiking trips. Sometimes these stories teetered on the edge of believability."[2] Van der Hoeven stated unequivocally, "There is a desire by these guys to have a good story to tell. They are dying to be interesting. Whether the story is made up or not isn't important. What is important is being entertaining."[3]

A core brand idea was starting to develop. These guys that the Dos Equis team found appealing weren't the trendsetters, and they weren't individualistic enough to completely stand out from the rest of the crowd. No, these guys were part of the group, but they were an important part of the group. They were the ones who were—and sought to be—interesting. They were the ones with the funny story, the incredible story—the ones who could hold court with tales of love and adventure. They were the ones who absolutely had to be included in the group. Without their presence, their stories, and their ability to share these stories with others, the group would be missing a key component, the glue that kept the group and their nights out fascinating. These guys were the ones whom Dos Equis wanted to romance.

Dos Equis saw an opening. The brand team would focus its efforts on differentiating itself almost exclusively on the brand's extrinsics—focusing its message on an emotional benefit and a mysterious personality. They would let the core emotional idea subtly communicate the brand's mysterious origins, unique taste, and Mexican heritage. The Dos Equis personality would differentiate the brand from both the sophisticated proposition of higher-end beers like Heineken and the slapstick message of domestic beers like Bud Light. Dos Equis would "win" an emotional benefit, one focused on the concept of *interesting*.

An "Interesting" Proposition

But what exactly did "interesting" mean? How should they communicate it in a crowded beer category? Given its small size, there was no way that Dos Equis could purchase the amount of national advertising media of larger brands, so the marketing team's message would have to break through to their consumer without the benefit of heavy media weights. "We were going to flip the traditional beer message on its head," said Rivas. "Instead of showing beer drinkers in humorous situations, the brand would say, 'You lead an interesting life and have a philosophy of living the most interesting life you can. We at Dos Equis share that philosophy.'" If the existing messaging to twenty-something men was defined by "babes, parties, and tailgating," Dos Equis would appeal to a core consumer whose biggest fear was the fear of being boring.

In one of what would be many of the departures from traditional beer category advertising, they wouldn't showcase that twenty-something man engaging in interesting activities. Rather, Milmoe said, "We didn't want them to necessarily see themselves, but rather say 'That guy is interesting.' We would want to try to tap into a user mind-set that says, 'I need to have experiences like that—that is who I need to be.'" The communication would center around one man, aptly nicknamed the Most Interesting Man in the World (MIM), who would represent intrigue and mystery. He would hint from being from Mexico, but certainly not overcommunicate it. More important, this man would engage in a number of interesting experiences designed to pique the user's attention. The team just needed to figure out who the MIM was.

He would not be someone young like the user Dos Equis wanted to attract—he would be older. As Milmoe explained, "We found that younger characters lacked authenticity. If they were that young, they didn't have credibility to have lived that much of an interesting life." The team also didn't want the brand to make the users feel insecure—which might happen if the communication depicted someone their age having these incredibly interesting experiences. Therefore, an older person would be the MIM. The team looked all over the United States until, as van der Hoeven said, "All of sudden we find this dusty grey headshot of this guy who captures everything we are looking for. [He] was perfect."

The actor, Jonathan Goldsmith, was a self-described Russian Jew from the Bronx. "He obviously wasn't overtly Mexican," said van der Hoeven, "but he had a weathered feel and seemed like he had been around the block." Milmoe added, "He was someone who our consumer could appreciate and aspire to be like when they were his age. He was like that cool uncle who shows up at family functions. He wasn't a threat and wouldn't be at our consumer's table at the bar, but he was someone who *they* would want to go over and meet."

Although the team was excited about the campaign and about their MIM, some in Heineken's management team weren't sure. Says van der Hoeven, "Sometimes who you envision being this individual and who it ends up being are completely different. Our management was under the impression that it would be a James Bond/Jason Bourne type character." They weren't getting that. In fact, Goldsmith could have been James Bond's father.

The other controversial element of the campaign was the ending line. As scripted, the MIM would look at the camera and state, "I don't always drink beer, but when I do, I prefer Dos Equis." Wait a minute. Would the MIM actually say that he didn't always drink beer? Think about other brand communications. Do any of them give you an out? Do any of them say, "Hey, we know you don't always use this category, but when you do, use our brand"? This was a radically different thought. The MIM was going to admit that his drink of choice wasn't *always* Dos Equis. Rivas added, "If he drank Dos Equis all the time, he wouldn't be as interesting. He had to be authentic and honest. His whole life goes *well beyond* Dos Equis. Dos Equis plays a very minor role in the grand scheme of things." Thus this simple line challenged conventional thinking, but it would create a bond of trust with the Dos Equis consumer and add to the brand's coolness.

The team ultimately convinced their management to move forward with the campaign, and it launched in eight southwestern markets on a tiny budget. Despite the small budget, it made a splash. Consumers began talking. The team saw lots of Internet chatter. Sales in those markets went up by double digits. According to Rivas, industry advertising evaluator Millward Brown revealed that the spot tested in the top 5 percent of all time among its database of seventy thousand television commercials tested. The results were so strong that plans were immediately made to introduce the MIM to the rest of the United States.

From Regional Success to National Exposure

New brand director Paul Smailes would be tasked with launching the campaign nationally while still not losing momentum in the regional markets. Smailes saw his task this way: "We had a nice blank canvas for the brand that would really enable us to introduce it to the entire country who hadn't been exposed to the Most Interesting Man idea."[4] He would take the campaign and extend it into a 360-degree marketing program that would surround drinkers looking to lead a more interesting life. This included social media activation, in-store activation, a traveling show (The Most Interesting Show in the World), and other proprietary sponsorships. However, none of these activation tools would feature the MIM. Dos Equis kept him guarded and mysterious, using him only in direct-to-user communications.

The country became fascinated: what would the Most Interesting Man do next? It wasn't just beer users who wanted to get close to the brand. Distributors and retailers also wanted more product and more promotion, anxious to leverage the unique excitement behind Dos Equis. According to Smailes, "We really found that we were able to expand our footprint in stores with additional packages and bring out a new Amber flavor. Our connection with the consumer was driving our business partners to also get behind the brand."

The numbers over a five-year period were amazing. According to Heineken internal data, from the time of the regional campaign launch in 2007 through fall 2011, brand awareness had increased some 47 percent, and the brand saw its case volume more than double. On Facebook, Dos Equis became the first beer brand to achieve one million likes. And in fall 2012, *Saturday Night Live* featured a spoof commercial for "Tres Equis" featuring guest host Joseph Gordon-Levitt as the son of the Most Interesting Man (played by Jason Sudekis).

CREATING A BOND

The Dos Equis story illustrates the most important piece in the development of a brand-consumer relationship: the ability to take what originates as a product with attributes and create a personified brand that a particular consumer will find appealing. Think of the analogy with your own relationships. You probably know your type (or at least think you do); you have a pretty good sense of the type of person you're attracted to, the type of person who's attracted to you, the type of people you choose—and, more important, don't choose—as friends. Our relationships (particularly our romantic ones) are sparked by attraction. At the most surface level, we're attracted by another's physical attributes—eyes, hair, face, body, and so on. Many a relationship has started based on sheer physical attraction. However, for a relationship to become anything lasting, we must go beyond the physical, to personalities, commonalities, emotional connections, and the potential for shared experiences.

Brand-consumer relationships follow a similar trajectory. Marketers often make the mistake of thinking of consumers in terms of their "physical" attributes—their age, gender, income level, education level, and so on—without going deeper. Ask a junior brand manager who her consumer is, and she will usually describe him in these demographic terms. Likewise, consumers often encounter brands as collections of qualities or attributes that bundle up to provide some functional benefit for them—or don't. For those brands with which they don't perceive a connection, consumers will feel little emotion; these are brands that serve a need and can easily be replaced by something else that is "close enough" if that is more convenient.

But the stronger brand-consumer relationships, like genuine human relationships, go beyond the physical and practical. Brand managers seeking these relationships start describing consumers in terms of their *psychographics*—their attitudes, beliefs, hobbies, and passions. In the strongest brand-consumer relationships, the consumer also experiences (and describes) the brand less in terms of what it does for her than in terms of how it makes her *feel*. Strong brands take on personalities that are not only appealing to consumers but aspirational as well. In my experience, romances with the strongest brands result in the users' actually feeling that the brand was "designed for them."

Such was the case with Dos Equis. The brand team achieved success by truly understanding the consumer with whom they wanted to engage. They successfully built up from the physical product attributes and functional benefits to a series of emotional and social benefits, which they then communicated through a unique brand personality. The winning brand proposition—*interesting*—was both complex and easy to grasp.

In the remainder of this chapter, we will focus on understanding our consumer in order to build upon physical product attributes and develop a holistic brand proposition that will truly connect. Specifically, we'll discuss the creation of a proposition with a meaningful emotional and social benefit that is manifested through an attractive personality.

Personality, connection, relationship—it all starts when we understand and know our consumers. So how do we get to know them? The hot trend in marketing is the focus on leveraging analytics, the hope being that "big data" will solve all our problems and turbocharge all our marketing efforts. The current mad rush to big data reminds me of watching my six-year-old twin daughters' softball team in action. Someone hits the ball, and all nine players on the field frantically run after it. No one is covering first base. The game breaks down. In my view, the analytics obsession of both the practitioner and academic wings of the marketing industry reflects a similar mistake—it's distracting us from the actual game.

There's no magic bullet that will transform marketing. Although analytics represents a powerful set of new tools that certainly have their place in the marketing world, it's no panacea. By definition, data are impersonal and rarely enable us to understand consumers at their core. Furthermore, analytics measures only what we ask it to measure. Regarding Dos Equis, Kersten Rivas put it this way: "If we had just gone by the segmentation studies and grouped consumers based upon an inventory of likes and dislikes, we would have never noticed the 'interesting' idea. We would have never been able to get any depth behind it. The idea was a very social and conversational idea. Those aren't going to come up using big data or analytics." Consumers are more than numbers, and they are more than surveys. Big data doesn't tell us how to reach a consumer at the emotional or soulful level. Big data doesn't socialize. To truly cement a relationship, you have to converse, and being a good brand steward requires that you listen to conversations. If you don't, you will miss the special moment, the key insight, the magic ingredient that cements the potential for "romance."

The Dos Equis team went looking for that magic ingredient. They got to know the fears and dreams of the brand's potential consumers, and out of these they created something that was inherently appealing. It is an important lesson for any marketer to take away—a classic example of paying attention to both the forest and the trees. Numbers and models can give us a place to start, but if we get hung up on them, we're going to miss the moment that will reveal to us something so critical and so important to our potential users that we lose our best chance of establishing a meaningful connection with them.

YOUR DISTINCTIVE CONSUMER

There are certain consumers who simply fit better with our brand than with other options. We know that consumers choose brands, but choosing goes both ways: brands should also try to concentrate on those consumers with whom they want to have a relationship. These are the users who will value the relationship so much that they will accept no substitute. They will resist the need to "cheat" when a competitor offers a coupon or other compelling offer. The most important ones will have the ability to influence other consumers: their recommendation will serve to persuade their friends and relations. These particular consumers, whom I'll refer to as *influencers*, are key to a brand's overall health. Their influence inspires and motivates others. If all works out to plan, many of them eventually become brand evangelists by preaching the good news of the brand in subtle or overt ways.

As an example of identifying and marketing to a brand's influencers, take my own experience on Powerade. Recall that our strategy was for Powerade to focus its efforts on the next generation of sports drink users: teens entering the category. We could have stopped there. We could have tried to market our products to a general demographic population of teen sports drink users. But as you now know, creating a strong relationship requires more than just communicating to a general consumer demographic about surface-level product attributes. Demographics would give us a starting point, but we had to go beyond the physical. To really connect with teen boys in an emotional way as they entered the sports drink category, we had to appeal to a certain attitude or psychographic that they shared—an attitude that others would find appealing and gravitate toward.

Obviously, understanding sports would be critical. But more specifically we had to understand the underlying emotional connection that kids have with sports. Research showed that on an average high school campus, the top athletes were generally seen as the "big men on campus." (Ninety percent of young males indicated that the coolest kids were very good at sports.[5]) The athletes' opinions were followed: they were the designators of cool and were seen as leaders among their peers. In a typical high school community, they might not start a trend, but often their approval of emerging trends signaled which would succeed and which would fail. If they weren't behind you, then you weren't legitimate. Our goal was to engage in a strongly committed relationship with these guys, because if we could get them to feel passionately about the brand, their endorsement could potentially drive consumption among their friends. If a brand can engage in a relationship with a consumer who inspires others, then there is a good chance that the brand will be accepted by that influencer's followers.

Our influencer strategy would focus like a laser on getting that small, deeply important group of high school sports leaders not just to engage in a relationship with the brand but to become brand evangelists to other kids, including their younger brothers. Let Gatorade be their dad's sports drink. We would be *their* sports drink.

PROVIDING EMOTIONAL AND SOCIAL BENEFITS

To connect emotionally with these guys, we had to understand the mentality of sports. This would enable us to deduce the potential needs that would be met by sports drinks. Two big questions needed to be answered: Why do kids and teens play sports, and what do they derive from it emotionally?

At its most basic level, sports represents a transition from childhood to adulthood. For teen boys, it is the first time that their masculinity is put on display. Sports teach boys the concept of winning and losing, but it also teaches them key lessons around perseverance, helps increase their confidence, and rewards effort and hard work. Linking the brand to the key emotional drivers of teen sports would be the way that Powerade would establish a relationship with these boys. It would be critical for the brand to become part of their athletic routine. We would position the brand as an essential, visible piece of sports equipment that would always be on the field. Just as ball players needed their gloves, swimmers needed their goggles, and sprinters needed their running shoes, our teen consumers would need their Powerade.

Think about getting to this emotional connection with your brand. Similar to finding the right functional benefit, the way to discover a differentiated emotional benefit is to discover something you can own that connects logically to an emotional benefit. How?

First, *find the emotional opening*. Consumers will share similar functional needs and will enter a category to ensure that those needs are fulfilled. The key for a brand in that category is to link that functional benefit to an overarching emotional need that is driving the functional need. There is a strong emotionally based consumer need in almost every category. Your job is to find it. It won't be obvious; going beyond functionality is hard—it requires higher-order thinking. Talking to, listening to, and engaging with your ideal consumer will be essential in determining a compelling emotional space in which your brand can differentiate itself.

Second, *map out and thoroughly explore the emotional space you've identified*. It goes without saying that people are complex. To effectively connect them to a brand, we must understand the multiple ways their emotions are tied in to a category. Employing specific qualitative techniques, such as traditional laddering exercises, will help bring out consumers' true emotional feelings toward the category. Ask them to further elaborate on a functional benefit: "OK, so this product quenches your thirst. What does that mean to you?" If they say, "By quenching my thirst, it enables me to stay focused in the game longer." Then ask, "If you stay focused in the game longer, what does that do for you?" They may say, "It means I am giving my best effort." Then ask, "If you are giving your best effort, what does that mean?" They may say, "It means I can contribute more to our chances of success and give us a better chance to win." Then ask, "If you contribute more to a team's chance of success, what does that mean?" and so on. It is an iterative process. Keep laddering upward until you have a robust benefit structure that corresponds to the initial functional benefits found by the consumer.

Finally, *look outside your category.* Use similar categories to gain insights around how consumers connect emotionally within a need state. For example, to explore the brand's positioning as a "piece of athletic gear," the Powerade brand team spent a lot of time watching other athletic equipment providers—Nike, Adidas, and Rawlings—to better understand how to relate to the athletic pursuits of our teen males.

Everything Powerade did would focus like a laser around the young "sports–active" male influencer. This focus was at the absolute heart of the Powerade brand strategy. If the leaders in the high school sports community endorsed the brand, we would have a better chance of their teammates adopting the brand. The brand team envisioned a scenario where drinking a Powerade would serve as a *badge* that for the user said something about "me as an athlete." A badge is a symbol that tells the world something about the "user." If Powerade established badge value and became a symbol which indicated that the user took athletics seriously, the brand's social value would be enhanced. In other words, the brand wanted not just to appeal emotionally to the young sports–active male but also to aid in enhancing his social status among his friends and peers.

The social power that a brand can bring to a user remains underestimated by most marketers. Brands can act as a badge that says something to others about what the user believes in, the user's attitudes and opinions, and ultimately who he or she is as an individual. The Dos Equis team started with a mission— to encourage their core influencers, who were already perceived as interesting, to become even more interesting. Their followers, who also desired to be more interesting, saw Dos Equis as an entry into the conversation. In their minds, if the influencers were drinking Dos Equis and had accepted it as a brand, then why wouldn't they?

Taking the discussion back to the relationship model, the key to this chain of exchanges and influences—of relationships—lies in our sociability. As humans, we are social creatures. We grow when we interact with others; more than that, we must interact or else we cease to be fully functional humans. This is a basic, powerful truth. Dos Equis just wants to be a small part of that interaction. It wants to be the brand that gives the user confidence to know that he is, in fact, interesting and can engage with others.

Note also that the Dos Equis team hangs on the words "STAY THIRSTY, *my friends*," indicating that we should always be seeking out our next adventure and never rest on our laurels. That our quest should be to live a life on which, when we are the age of the MIM, we can look back with few regrets, knowing that we lived our lives to the fullest. Dos Equis wants to be a small reminder that we have choices throughout our lives and that we can, if we desire, choose to live a life that pushes the boundaries. Rivas noted, "For our consumer, material things mean less, and experiences mean more. They don't want to make it up. They want to experience it and live it. We're going to be a brand that walks the walk." It is that kind of inspiration that separates the strongest brands from the rest of the pack and demonstrates a social benefit that a brand can provide.

Recall the concept of badge value. If a brand enables a consumer to make a statement about himself or herself, that consumer will ultimately find more value in that brand and may pay more for it than for a brand that doesn't offer that same social currency. Let's revisit the smartwater brand to see this in action.

DEVELOPING A BADGE

Since its inception in 1996, smartwater had been changing the way that the bottled water category had been defined. Prior to its launch, bottled water represented the ultimate commodity. There was little difference in any of the brands that made up the category. The consumer perception, for the most part, was that water was water, and although there were brands within the category, they felt more like commodities. Most of the packaging was similar—plastic, soft-drink-like bottles, blue labels, and vague references to some spring—and there was little advertising. As a result, the category had morphed into one in which the players with the strongest distribution (Coke with Dasani and Pepsi with Aquafina) generated the strongest share.

With its smartwater brand, glacéau was dramatically changing the way the category interacted with its consumer base. Introduced regionally in the late 1990s, smartwater had ridden the wave of a bottled water category that was reaping the benefits of sweeping consumer changes and category growth. The wave was driven in part by a heavy dose of media exposure on how important water was to one's health. At the time, the bottled water consumer was being bombarded with news and health stories on the need to stay hydrated. Women, who represented a significant proportion of the user base, were hearing that more water intake led to a cleaner, more hydrated body, which had benefits ranging from keeping weight down to eliminating dry skin. All of a sudden, you saw women everywhere carrying a bottle of water in their hand. Walking down the street, going into meetings, or stepping into the gym, women were carrying bottled water just like they were carrying their purses. The water bottle was actually morphing into an accessory—something with which to be seen. And smartwater had something going for it that would enable it to become the ultimate accessory.

Previously, in response to the sameness that greeted him in the bottled water aisle, smartwater developer Darius Bikoff had decided that packaging (along with the differentiated functional benefit of smart hydration) was one of the few ways to differentiate his brand. As a result, he approached famed architect and product developer Philippe Starck to design the smartwater bottle. Starck had designed everything from juicers to hotel interiors to yachts, and would now design a bottle that was tall, thin, and quite modern in appearance—nothing like the other water containers that dominated store shelves.

The brand leveraged these attributes to grow the smartwater brand. They had a unique name, smartwater, which was very appealing to the consumer. Who doesn't want to be smart? They had a product makeup that was different from other bottled water both in the way that it was made and in the way that it was packaged. And the packaging, which looked like nothing else in the category, could lay a foundation for a strong emotional benefit that would ultimately enhance the brand's reputation.

Given that women were carrying around bottled water as an accessory, why not hop on to this trend? As Matt Kahn, former smartwater senior VP of marketing, explains, "We had the perfect fashion accessory. It was iconic packaging. On one hand, the straight bottle was so simplistic and unpretentious, but at the same time had a sleekness that represented something stylish for consumers."[6] Similar to our wanting Powerade to be an essential piece of sports equipment on the field, Kahn's objective was for smartwater always to be in the hands of the "in" crowd as they went about their daily lives. The brand's goal would be to become an icon that said, "Taking care of myself is important to me, and smartwater helps me look and feel my best."

Like Powerade, smartwater had developed a powerful influencer strategy. The team had defined the smartwater influencer as the woman who was perceived as extremely conscious of her health, yet who also displayed a keen sense of style. She obviously would need to be interested in the brand's functional benefit of smart hydration. Equally as important would be for her to be seen as a leader within her peer group—she was the one who others aspired to be, especially around the areas of fitness and fashion. If others saw her with the brand, they would be more likely to adopt it as their own. The strategy would focus on getting the influencer to see smartwater as a badge that said something about who she was and what she was about—much like a particular brand of purse or scarf.

LADDERING UP

How could smartwater create a badge? The key was to establish a connection to the influencer so that she would discover that the brand was more than just water. We've seen that the most successful brands start with the product itself. But they don't stop there. In the context of the relationship, carefully building up to a personality provides the means to consistently communicate and build the brand's reputation. Let's look at building the brand's reputation more closely in the context of the relationship between brand and influencer.

Functional and Emotional Benefits

Recall that we start with the product itself, specifically its *features and attributes*. If we take our smartwater example, we find that its product attributes include the sleek, tall bottle; the word "smartwater" written in lowercase letters; the humorous anecdotes on the package; the added electrolytes; and even the vapor distillation process. Now we need to translate those attributes into *functional benefits*. In human terms, functional benefits would be what a person does for his or her partner. It's what he or she physically provides for the other (for example, being a companion, doing a favor, giving a hug, and so on). In our smartwater example, functional brand benefits include efficient hydration, great taste, and being an essential component of the consumer's health and wellness routine.

Emotional benefits are defined as how the brand makes the influencer feel. They must be inextricably linked to the brand's functional benefits. This is where the brand must establish a deeper connection with the influencer. Now we are getting into fertile relationship territory. How does the brand make the user feel when she uses the brand? If you've done your homework and truly engaged with the influencer to understand her passion points, emotional needs, and reason for wanting to engage with your brand, you should be able to discover the emotional benefits. In the smartwater example, they include giving the consumer self-confidence in knowing that she is stylish and *feeling* that she is doing something good for her body by purifying it.

Social Benefits

But we can't just stop there. As we discussed, the social component to brands is essential. The ability of the brand to provide social benefits to the influencer, either by serving as talk value in a social setting or as a badge that tells others something about who she is as an individual is critical to the brand-consumer relationship. Let's call this capacity a brand's *social cachet*. It's crucial that we ask ourselves, How will we enhance the brand's social cachet?

One way is to *provide story value*. As the Dos Equis campaign shows, we all want to be interesting. We want stories. The Dos Equis communication campaign had such richness and depth associated with it that it was creating a tremendous amount of word of mouth among its most sought-after consumers. Consumers were gladly passing along MIM stories and engaging in a rich dialogue about the MIM and Dos Equis. The very stories that Dos Equis was associating with the MIM served to enhance the social cachet of the Dos Equis brand.

Another route to social cachet is to *be someone with whom others want to be seen*. This is the "coolness" variable. How do you know when something is cool? It can seem so arbitrary—trying to describe coolness is somewhat akin to the classic description of pornography: I can't articulate to you what it is, but I know it when I see it. Coolness can't be measured. It can't necessarily be dictated. It can, however, be inspired. The way a brand looks, sounds, feels, or tastes can add to its inherent coolness factor and ultimately contribute to attracting the influencer. As we'll see later, whom a brand associates with also plays a role in enabling it to graduate to an entity others want to be seen with and to talk about.

But before we can fully understand a brand's social cachet, we have to ensure that its *personality* is compatible with the influencer. Coolness is also driven by a brand's personality. Remember Jennifer Aaker and her brand personality work, discussed in Chapter One? Brand personalities dictate the tone and mood of consumer messaging. The *Merriam-Webster Dictionary* defines *personality* as "characteristics that distinguish an individual or a nation or group; especially: the totality of an individual's behavioral and emotional characteristics." Our personality identifies us and contributes heavily to making us the unique beings that we are. You know the personalities that you are attracted to and the ones that you find abhorrent. When it comes to brands, a personality must be developed that not only helps in identifying the brand but also serves a major role in attracting a certain consumer. The influencer must feel that a brand is for "someone like me."

In fact, as we saw at Coke, the more a consumer feels as though a brand is "for someone like me," the greater the likelihood that she will purchase the brand. Part of this involves having compatible personalities. It's true in the realm of human relationships, too: the way you connect emotionally with another individual and grow your relationship has a lot to do with how your personalities appeal to one another.

Likewise, through their look, their messaging, and their tone, brands have personalities that will be appealing to a select group of influencers. A brand whose personality is embraced by the right consumer will be more likely to create brand loyalty and ultimately brand love. Choosing and successfully projecting the right personality can radically change the brand's trajectory.

• • •

Take the classic case of Miller Lite, at the time referred to as Lite Beer from Miller, a beer whose personality enabled it to transform and define an entire beer subcategory. When Miller Brewing Company acquired the first nationally distributed light beer, Meisterbrau Light, few thought that it would become anything more than a small niche beer for a small slice of the category—female beer drinkers looking for fewer calories. But Miller had other plans. It believed that the renamed Lite Beer from Miller could become a large, mainstream beer. To do that, it would have to bond with the largest segment of beer drinkers—those blue-collar guys who saw beer as an essential ingredient of male camaraderie. This was no small task—how do you get a hard-core thirty-something beer drinker to embrace a beer with low calories that was perceived as being for women? The conventional wisdom was that the marketing team had zero chance of success.

Scott Miller, former creative director for McCann Erickson (Miller's advertising agency), describes it this way: "It was 'Mission Impossible.' Beer always has been and always will have a strong badge value associated with it. What you drink says something directly about you. At the time, if your 'bar call' wasn't Budweiser, you had to explain it. Your masculinity was on the line."[7] In other words, if you were a tough blue-collar guy, there was no way that you would order anything that was perceived as a light beer. The McCann team would have to completely change consumer perception so that a guy could order Lite Beer from Miller and still be seen as a "real man."

The team got to work. They found that for blue-collar males, beer was an integral part of an afternoon hanging out with the guys in the bar and watching football. But there was one negative associated with beer in this context: it filled you up. These guys didn't want a bloated feeling to curb what would be an afternoon of fun with the boys at the bar. Functionally, lower calories might be an answer. Not because it would result in a better figure or better health, but because the consumer would be able to drink more and be one of the guys for a longer period of time.

The McCann team had found the functional benefit, but how would they connect this to an emotional benefit and an authentic personality? They decided to personify Lite Beer from Miller as "your buddy at the bar" and used rugged former athletes to act as pitchmen. At the time, active professional athletes were prohibited from endorsing alcoholic beverages, but for Miller, former athletes would fit just fine. Ex-athletes were tough: they played the game the way it was supposed to be played, and represented bruised warriors who had made their contributions on the field. They had "hung them up" and were now enjoying the fruits of their labor by being able to relax and just be one of the guys at the bar.

But what was needed was authenticity around the brand's personality that transcended the spokesperson model. Scott adds, "The brand had to man up. We had to make it acceptable for one of these guys to feel comfortable ordering Lite Beer from Miller at the bar." So they called upon ex-athletes like Dick Butkus, Bubba Smith, and Joe Frazier not just to pitch Lite Beer from Miller but to get in heated arguments at the bar as to whether the brand "tasted great" or was "less filling." The brand now had a new personality—one that was tough but that also had a sense of humor. In short, the brand *became* your buddy at the bar. The approach was a successful one: the brand was embraced by the critical blue-collar male beer drinker. It had become one of the guys. It also enabled Lite Beer from Miller to become the second-largest beer in the United States, trailing only Budweiser, from the early 1980s to 1994.[8] Of note, the McCann Erickson campaign was also acknowledged as the eighth best campaign of the twentieth century by *Advertising Age*.[9]

Your Unique Personality

Lite Beer from Miller provides great insight into how to create a brand personality that resonates with your ideal consumer. There are two main principles to keep in mind as you develop that personality.

First, *ensure that the personality is not just appealing but inspirational to the consumer.* The key question that must be asked here is, Who is the type of person your influencer would like to hang out with? It's not just about being acceptable; it's about being compelling. In Lite Beer from Miller's case, "your buddy at the bar" was something that the ideal consumer would embrace. He could relate to a buddy. A buddy is someone whom you can pal around with as well as someone who will support you. Lite Beer from Miller's personality made it seem like one of the guys. If your influencer can't or won't embrace your brand's personality, then you either have the wrong personality or are focusing on the wrong influencer.

Second, *ensure that the brand's personality will be evident in every consumer touchpoint.* We'll discuss this in more detail later, but keep in mind that a brand's logo, packaging, communications, colors, and associations are all ways that brands communicate their personality to their consumers. If any of these are inconsistent, the chances are greater that the consumer will discount the brand as inauthentic and not bond with it. If Lite Beer from Miller had engaged in a campaign that only mentioned tasting great and being less filling, without the ex-athletes arguing about it in a bar, it never would have succeeded. The ex-athletes and their loud, humorous actions became the brand's persona. Everything communicates. You must ensure that every message the consumer gets from the brand is using the same personality and tone. (Fast-forward to today, and the renamed Miller Lite is struggling. It abandoned the masculine, "your buddy at the bar" positioning for an "edgier" message similar to category leader Bud Light. A few years ago, Scott Miller went back and researched why the brand he had worked on had fallen on hard times. He found that Miller Lite had "lost its masculine identity" and was now considered a generic light beer, relying on its awareness, distribution, and heritage.)

Think about the brands we've discussed so far. Each of them has a strong personality. Dos Equis is seen as mysterious, aspirational, and, most important, interesting. Powerade has a cutting-edge confidence and attitude that, though bordering on cockiness, is still authentic and deeply intense. Taking it further, Powerade might be personified as that kid who never wants to stop playing, the one whose love of sports transcends just the game on the field, the one who is always seeking to elevate his performance. In smartwater's case, the personality is about being more than looking good on the surface. There's no superficiality to it. smartwater's packaging—not just the sleek bottle but the witty descriptive packaging copy as well—helps to communicate its personality, which could be described as *modern, youthful, unpretentious, confident, stylish, humorous*, and *trustworthy*.

The Essence of the Brand

Product attributes, functional and emotional benefits, social cachet, and personality all lead to the brand's *essence*. The essence is captured as an enduring phrase that describes the brand. This is that *one thing* that we discussed earlier. This is truly what the brand owns. For Volvo it is "safe cars." For Disney it is "family magic." For Coca-Cola it is "authentic happiness." For Wal-Mart it is "low prices every day." For Jack Daniels it is "American masculinity." The brand essence for smartwater might be "helps me look and feel my best." Now, being a younger brand, smartwater is nowhere near these other brands in establishing this essence. This takes time and years of consistent effort. But for the strongest brands, that one simple phrase, when it emerges, will result in every influencer's knowing exactly what the brand is.

To encapsulate the concept of benefit laddering, let's look at a *brand pyramid* that illustrates laddering up from product attributes all the way to a core essence (Figure 3.1). Along the

Figure 3.1 Laddering Up Benefits

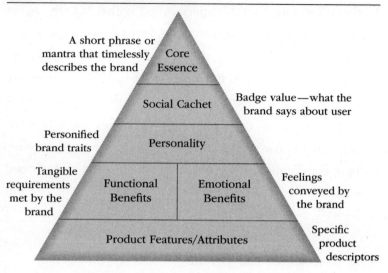

path to the core essence, we see functional and emotional benefits, a personality, and social cachet.

Let's also look at this brought to life with a hypothetical smartwater brand pyramid, as shown in Figure 3.2.

What do you notice about the smartwater brand pyramid? It's logical. It's focused. And, most important, it all fits together. A strong brand will create logical steps that take consumers from the bare-bones product attributes into something much, much deeper. It is within this context that we will begin seeding the relationship with our influencer. She won't discover the depth of our brand immediately, but what we will put out there will be compelling enough that the consumer will become interested in pursuing our brand further. It will be our first attempt at "charming" the influencer. But first we have to bring to life this dynamic persona that is our brand. We achieve this by finding the right associations.

Figure 3.2 smartwater Brand Pyramid

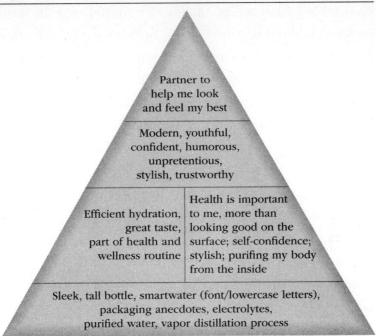

Partner to
help me look
and feel my best

Modern, youthful,
confident, humorous,
unpretentious,
stylish, trustworthy

Efficient hydration,
great taste,
part of health and
wellness routine

Health is important
to me, more than
looking good on the
surface; self-confidence;
stylish; purifing my body
from the inside

Sleek, tall bottle, smartwater (font/lowercase letters),
packaging anecdotes, electrolytes,
purified water, vapor distillation process

FINDING AN ASSOCIATION

Think about an important person in your life. Did you know
something about him before you actually met? Whom he associated with, what his hobbies were, where he hung out—all
these provide some insight into a person you may know about
but haven't yet gotten to know.

Likewise, a brand's associations, context, and reputation
affect the way consumers view that brand before they've actually experienced it. *Brand associations*, defined as anything that
links a brand with a third party, can range from Tostitos' sponsorship of the Fiesta Bowl (linking the brand to football and

tailgating parties) to Michelle Obama's wearing a White House/Black Market dress on *The View* (introducing the retail outlet to millions of Americans).[10] Brands partner with other entities because we want to borrow those entities' equity or personality (or both) and align it with our brand.

Think about it from a relationship standpoint. In human terms, a brand's associations give consumers clues as to whom the brand hangs out with, its hobbies, and its interests. For brands, associations clearly bring risks. Depending on whom the brand associates with, it may immediately either gain or lose key consumer segments. A brand with associations that reinforce its core message will have a much greater chance of breaking through and getting the influencer's attention. The choices that a marketing team makes in this arena play a significant role. Such was the case with smartwater and its national launch.

The Brand Personified

In early 2005, as he was driving on the Van Wyck freeway past the early morning shadows of Shea Stadium, Matt Kahn, then a brand director for smartwater, was deep in thought contemplating the first-ever national marketing campaign for the smartwater brand. As a former brand manager at Coca-Cola, he had received a baptism by fire when it came to big marketing events and associations. The Olympics, the Super Bowl, the Grammy Awards, and *American Idol* were all among the arsenal of associations that The Coca-Cola Company had at its disposal to launch brands. But Kahn now worked for a small, upstart, entrepreneurial group at glacéau, where resources were tight, and nimbleness and efficiency, rather than big marketing spends, were the norm. Kahn, however, wanted to take a risk and utilize a celebrity strategy as smartwater expanded its distribution nationally. He felt that because celebrities set trends and get a lot of free press, they made sense within the glacéau spending strategy. He explains, "As a brand that wanted to be a fashion accessory, being in the hands of the right celebrity could do wonders. For a brand that didn't have the kind of money to create a large national television campaign, it would be a way to efficiently seed the brand's reputation."

The key, however, would be to find the right celebrity to represent the brand. After all, the entire purpose of the celebrity strategy would be to borrow preexisting equity that the celebrity had and transfer that to the brand. Kahn laid out a few key criteria in securing the right smartwater spokesperson—a spokesperson who could lay a foundation for consumer relationships at the national level:

- Most important, she would need to credibly reflect the brand's message: she would need to be seen as someone who was healthy and in shape.
- She would need to have a personality that was real and approachable, not superficial and standoffish.
- She would need to personally embrace the brand and everything it stood for.

A number of names were considered. They were all high-profile "A-list" Hollywood actresses. All, on the surface, seemed to meet the criteria that had been set out. But there was one who stood out above the rest as the best fit for the brand. Kahn described the reasons: "First, she was seen as approachable. She represented the girl next door, but was still very attractive and stylish. It was an interesting dichotomy. She obviously took care of her body and, as a result, looked much younger than she actually was. This helped to reinforce the fact that smartwater was really the first bottled water to emphasize that it contained a blend of minerals. She was healthy and fit—smartwater played a small role in that."

It didn't hurt that she was one of the hottest celebrities in Hollywood, with a significant arsenal of hit movies and the number-one television show *Friends* under her belt. It also was important that she was one of the world's most photographed celebrities. Of course, even if you don't remember the campaign, you now know that Jennifer Aniston was the person smartwater chose to represent the brand to the world. If the brand could effectively partner with her and she would embrace the brand and carry it around with her as an accessory, the strategy would be in place.

Kahn says, "Jennifer Aniston truly loved the brand. She went out of her way to carry it with her as an accessory [and to] get pictured with the brand more regularly, and made more appearances than she was required to by her contract." In establishing the brand's reputation on a national level, she was perfect. Kahn acknowledges that Aniston enhanced the smartwater personality: "What appealed to us about Jen was that she was aspirational and yet seemed approachable. She was stylish, but had classic taste in fashion. She worked hard to keep fit, and while she took her acting craft seriously, she didn't take herself too seriously, which dovetailed nicely with the witty copy contained on our sleek package." In other words, Aniston enabled the brand to extend its accessory imagery and ultimately assist in creating a badge.

A robust print and outdoor campaign featuring Aniston was launched, and the consumer response was considerable. The brand received strong consumer increases on the following attitudinal statements: "Helps me look and feel my best," "A trusted brand," and "Stylish." More important, even though it had been launched many years after super premium water brands Evian and Fiji, smartwater became the number-one premium bottled water in America. In the worst economy since the Great Depression, which saw premium brands decline at significant rates, the investment behind growing smartwater's reputation resulted in double-digit growth year after year.[11]

Marrying Brand and Association

Obviously, a key to creating a strong brand reputation is determining ultimately how the brand pyramid will be communicated. Celebrities are just one of those ways. As we'll see later, associations can take many forms.

So how do you go about finding the right fit? If we think of this in a relationship context, the right associations should be those that align so well with the brand that the brand could be married to them. A great exercise that I've used many times is to create an alignment matrix between the brand and its potential association. In the alignment matrix, elements of the brand's positioning and character are compared with those of the intended association. Let's take smartwater's brand alignment with Jennifer Aniston. As we saw earlier, smartwater's emotional benefits, laddered up from its functional attributes and benefits, can be summarized as follows:

- I feel healthy
- Says something about who I am (badge value)
- Is about more than just looking good

The brand personality these suggest is

- Modern
- Sleek and stylish
- Unpretentious

Compare that to what is commonly perceived about the "Jennifer Aniston" brand attributes:

- Attractive
- Healthy and physically fit
- Sense of humor
- Trendsetter
- Regularly photographed/newsworthy
- Treats others well

And her personality:

- Girl next door
- Funny
- Unpretentious
- Approachable
- Friendly

Clearly Jennifer Aniston's attributes and personality closely match a personified smartwater. It made her a natural choice to represent the brand. Only by closely aligning the perception of the association with the brand's benefits, personality, and social cachet will we be able to transfer the equity from one to the other. But you have to be careful. Even if something aligns on paper, when it actually gets executed in the marketplace, it can turn out quite differently. Celebrities are human, and if a brand is too closely aligned with one, the brand reaps the consequences if a celebrity goes down in flames. Sometimes it makes more sense to create an association with an entity rather than a person.

For Powerade, we specifically decided that we would *not* use celebrities. Why? Gatorade utilized Michael Jordan and a host of other high-profile professional sports stars in its communication. Instead, we decided to springboard off The Coca-Cola Company's long-standing Olympic sponsorship to become the "Official Sports Drink of the Olympic Games," which established another differentiation from Gatorade. Whereas Gatorade was perceived as being the sports drink for professional athletes and sports leagues, Powerade would be associated with Olympic athletes, who, like our consumer, engaged in athletics for the love of the sport rather than the love of money.

Senior brand manager Larry Taman partnered with Nike to create a stable of Olympic hopefuls under the banner of the Powerade Athletic Club. Comprising up-and-coming athletes who weren't even guaranteed to make the Olympic team, the Powerade Athletic Club was a manifestation of the brand— young, hungry, with potential, but hardly proven.

Remember that product differentiator, "33% more carbo-hydrates," that we didn't know what to do with? The marketing team was finally able to link a benefit to that differentiator by using Olympic athletes. In an internal Coca-Cola survey, Olympic athletes indicated that they preferred more carbohydrates in their sports drinks. Brand manager Parra Vaughan took that survey result and linked it to the fact that Powerade had 33 percent more carbohydrates than Gatorade. This ultimately implied that Olympic athletes, the purest athletes in the world, preferred a sports drink formulation that was similar to Powerade and not Gatorade. The association with the Olympics helped communicate the message. In fact, the message that Olympians preferred more carbohydrates tested as being more persuasive than any Gatorade ad, including those featuring the great Michael Jordan.

● ● ●

In this chapter, we've explored ways to identify a brand's consumer type—the one who might be most interested in the brand's specific functional and emotional benefits, personality, social cachet, and essence. If the brand's proposition isn't clear, concise, authentic, or logically aligned with the influencer's needs, the relationship is doomed before it has even started. Remember, that first meeting is what it's all about. Our goal is to ensure that everything we can control is perfect for that initial meeting. If it doesn't go well, we can kiss any potential romance good-bye. It is essential to meet our influencer under the best possible circumstances. In the next chapter, we'll look at how to do just that.

4

MEET MEMORABLY

Think about when you met someone special in your life. For the record, my wife and I don't remember actually meeting. We kind of knew each other casually for a while and then started dating. We do, however, remember when we first started getting to know each other better. It started with a long conversation one day and evolved from there. Before we knew it, we had a connection.

The meeting of the brand and the consumer depends on a number of factors: the brand's perceived reputation prior to the meeting, previous "relationships" (the consumer's previous brand experiences and whether he or she is open to the brand's category), physical proximity (does the consumer have the actual opportunity to meet the brand?), and others. When a consumer initially "meets" or tries a brand is a huge step in starting a relationship. In human terms, if we meet someone, like him or her, and find that we have a lot in common, we'll develop a friendship (or more). Of course, if we find little in common, we'll stay in the acquaintance phase. The key for marketers is for the brand to meet influencers—those consumers who are inspirational to others within a category—in a way that lays the foundation for further interactions.

NICE TO MEET YOU

As a marketer you can only control so much, but there are ways to ensure that the initial meeting and subsequent early interactions go as well as possible. In this chapter, we'll look at four ways to create a memorable meeting with influencers:

- Make them feel special
- Make sure the context is right
- Stay consistent
- Establish intimacy

If a brand can achieve all four, the first meeting with the influencers will likely be a positive one.

Make Them Feel Special

When you've met someone and made a connection, you've undoubtedly communicated either consciously or subconsciously that there is something about that individual that appeals to you. Similarly, once you've identified your brand's type, you need to show those individuals that you think they are special.

Remember that Powerade's influencer was the "big man on campus"—that high school sports stud everyone wants to emulate. The brand wanted to convince that young athlete, still new to the sports drink category, that Powerade was an essential piece of sports equipment like their shoes or gloves. Everything—and I mean *everything*—we did was aimed to meet the needs of this group of influencers.

We sought them out. We got their opinions. Before the team launched any marketing initiative, any package, flavor, or communication for Powerade, we solicited the opinions of guys who were the athletic leaders in their school. They told us what was and what was not cool. We listened.

For example, ever wonder why sports drinks are available in a rainbow of neon colors? Research revealed that colors (and not the actual flavor or the flavor name) were the top driver of purchase when our influencer teen chose a sports drink. Bright, neon colors were seen as "intense" and "cutting edge." Powerade therefore developed a product line with bright neon colors—blue, purple, aqua, green. Prior to this, sports drinks came only in the traditional colors of yellow-green (lemon-lime), red (fruit punch), and orange. The influencers drove our decisions. We wanted to have the best product line possible when we met them.

So how did we introduce the brand to them for the first time?

Our first goal was to find the biggest athletes in every U.S. high school and introduce them to Powerade. Through pre-Internet search techniques using lists of top high school sports prospects for each of the major sports, we identified some one million top U.S. teen athletes. We introduced ourselves to them with a mail piece with the message "What's the Difference Between Draggin' Your Butt and Kickin' Some?" on the outside of the box. Inside the box, the answer, "The Right Equipment," appeared, along with our new "Powerflo" sports bottle and a Powerade coupon.

Think about this for a minute. Our influencer received something in the mail from Powerade (and these guys never received mail). Powerade had found *them*. All their friends didn't get one. In fact, it seemed that only those who excelled in sports received one. Powerade signaled that *they* were one of the top athletes in their school. Do you think that they might start having positive feelings toward Powerade? They had been chosen. The brand instantly gained a social currency: these guys, who weren't short on modesty to begin with, now had even more bragging rights.

At the same time that the Powerade direct mail campaign was hitting top high school athletes, high school coaches were being introduced to the brand. If a coach placed a Powerade vending machine in his gym or locker room, he was given significant amounts of Powerade-branded equipment, such as towels, coolers, and sports bottles to use on the field. In an age when school athletic budgets were being cut to the nub, additional team equipment was very welcome to these coaches. (The school's portion of vending machines sales also helped its athletic program.) From the athlete's perspective, the coach was tacitly endorsing the brand by using Powerade-branded equipment, serving the product on the field during practices, and having it available for athletes in the locker room.

We had introduced ourselves to the young sports–active male influencers in the right way—a way that spoke directly to them and made them feel special. As a result, we saw that among those under eighteen, brand loyalty between Powerade and Gatorade began to equalize.

Make Sure the Context Is Right

Of course the meeting environment is also critical. The consumer has to be in the right frame of mind, and the context has to be right. This is why we put such an emphasis on Powerade's placement in high school gyms. Likewise, once the smartwater team decided that their influencer was the fashion-forward, health-conscious young professional woman, they knew they had to introduce the brand to these women in the proper places. They began seeding the brand with these influencers in the places where they tended to congregate, sending product to the homes of women who ran hair salons, led yoga classes, and were personal trainers. The brand was also sent to the hottest gyms and dance clubs and every health store in Manhattan. It was given not just to the leadership of these organizations but to everyone involved in the operation. From the bodyguards at the trendy clubs to the front desk managers at the most popular gyms, smartwater would be seen everywhere that the "in crowd" was frequenting. Furthermore, the team arranged to hand out product samples at these locations (hiring and training staff to make the contact in the right way), so that gym and club patrons could likewise enjoy the product, but, more important, carry around the iconic bottle.

The smartwater team hoped that the initial influencers wouldn't just sample the product and stop—and they didn't. They quickly began to engage in a relationship with it, seeking it out, carrying it around, and talking about it. As a result, the brand began to be perceived differently from other bottled waters. In focus groups, influencers described their feelings about smartwater with words like "inspired" and "stylish," but also "accepting," "devoted," and "approachable." It was becoming "water plus"—and consumers found so much more value with smartwater than with other brands that they would pay extra for it.

As we've seen over the past few chapters, the smartwater consumer romance began for a number of reasons. First, the product's functional benefits appealed to the initial influencers. Second, these consumers felt that the brand truly was created for them; and through its look and feel, the brand began to create an emotional connection. Similar to what Powerade did for teen athletes, smartwater reached out to these highly influential women and gave them *attention*. It made them feel special. As a result, its social currency also increased. Influencers who had been made to feel special by an appealing brand talked up the brand with those who took their yoga classes or came to their hair salons. When the owners of New York's most popular clubs asked to start selling the brand (having been inundated with samples), they provided an implied endorsement.

Note that smartwater didn't communicate to the influencer in a typical bottled-water way. Because the bottle-as-accessory imagery had the potential to resonate with the influencers, the marketing communication around it had to resemble communication that one might employ for a blouse or purse or necklace. But it wasn't enough that the cool yoga teacher was carrying around the brand and felt a personal connection to it; smartwater also had to be ubiquitous in the right places so that it appeared as the "in" thing. The brand had to be available in the location where that yoga teacher worked (which was why lavish sampling was offered at the most popular clubs). The goal was not to sell a lot of volume in these locations, although that would be nice. Rather, it was to ensure that the budding brand reputation would be enhanced by being "seen" where influencers congregated. It gave the brand a broader yet still exclusive legitimacy.

Where you meet is almost as important as the meeting itself. The physical surroundings must be consistent with the brand's DNA. They must augment the brand message, never take away from it. Every business school teaches a basic brand-consumer-channel alignment strategy: the ultimate goal in bringing a brand to a consumer is creating an intersection between the user, the company's brand, and the channel through which the brand is sold. The marketing team must (1) understand and meet consumer needs with (2) the right brand proposition in (3) a setting that is *consistent* with the brand proposition. This is why you don't see Nike at Wal-Mart. Despite the fact that Nike could sell a lot of shoes at Wal-Mart, the Wal-Mart low price mentality doesn't fit with the Nike brand and would cause irreparable damage to Nike's consumer relationship. It would be much more costly than the short-term benefit Nike would receive from Wal-Mart availability.

Powerade and smartwater took this classic alignment strategy and gave it a twist and a boost: the initial channel or location was used both to establish and enhance the brand experience. In other words, the location didn't just *match* the brand proposition but *added* to it. It's a bit of a beneficial feedback loop: when effectively aligned, the influencer's needs, the brand proposition, and the setting all support and enhance one another.

Stay Consistent

Consider how many different ways a brand interacts with consumers. Think beyond just the product experience itself. Think about what the packaging says—its look, its colors, and its fonts. Think about where it is sold and what that store or channel communicates. Think about whom or with what a brand aligns. Think about its advertisements. Think about the types of shows or magazines where it's advertised. What does its price point say about the brand? Consider the promotions it runs and whom or what it might align with for a promotion. What does the name itself say about the brand? This is only a partial map of the numerous touchpoints a brand has with its audience. If these touchpoints aren't all consistent and focused on one core idea, especially when the influencer first takes notice, the brand is doomed.

Take product name as an example. I briefly worked on a brand that competed in what was, at the time, the energy drink category (prior to the emergence of Red Bull). The category was led by Mountain Dew, which had defined the category (found a way to win!) as liquid energy. It did this with a bright-yellow product that contained more caffeine than a typical soft drink (54mg versus 34mg for Coca-Cola). The category was all about the rush of energy that the product provided. Coke's competitive drink was the same color, had similar caffeine content, and was equally as potent. But Coke's product was named . . . *Mello* Yello. As hard as we tried to convince influencers that Mello Yello was an energy drink, the name completely violated the proposition. A good brand name isn't going to rescue an otherwise poorly designed product, but an ill-conceived one can saddle a brand with a burden that is difficult to overcome.

At Coke, it was beaten into our heads that *everything* communicates (notwithstanding the name/position mismatch of Mello Yello). And everything must communicate with an obsessive level of consistency (see Figure 4.1). Consider Disney. The Disney brand can be summarized in one word, "magic." Every time Disney communicates, the primary message is "magic." Whether you are at one of the parks, watching a movie, seeing Disney on Ice, or on a Disney cruise, the entire experience is all about magic. Disney cast members tell you to "Have a magical day" at every interaction in the parks. The Ritz-Carlton is famous for its pledge, "ladies and gentlemen serving ladies and gentlemen." There is an obsessive level of

Figure 4.1 Brand Reputation: Everything Communicates

consistency in everything the Ritz-Carlton does to make its guests feel pampered, providing them with an "unwavering commitment to service," as its website states. These brands are always consistent, and this consistency is crucial, especially when the consumer is first meeting the brand. It increases the brand's ability to break through and make a connection.

Establish Intimacy

Of course, within the context of the meeting, we have to get past the "hello" phase. This is critical. We have to share something with that consumer beyond the surface "nice-to-meet-you-and-move-on"—something that makes him or her stop, take notice, and want to learn more. We have to get to a deeper level and get there quickly.

Entrepreneur Janie Hoffman found herself in a situation where she wasn't just launching a new brand but launching a new subcategory. Furthermore, this extension was radically different from what existing users of that category expected. In fact, she wouldn't just have to get consumers to meet her new Mamma Chia brand health beverage; she would have to educate them and convince them to engage with something that was quite a departure from traditional beverages out there—a tall order to fill.

If there was ever a brand designed with the user's soul in mind, Mamma Chia is it. Hoffman had discovered chia seeds—which, thirty years ago, were the foundation of those wonderfully obnoxious chia pets, but which turn out to have excellent nutritional properties. Hoffman suffered from several autoimmune disorders and was always looking for foods to keep her body strong, often going from food to food in search of something to augment her already healthy diet. As Janie recalls, one day she was complaining to a friend about flax seeds, their limited shelf life, and the time and effort it took to grind them. The friend asked why she wasn't using chia instead. "She said chia seeds had no taste, were high in antioxidants, huge in omega-3, and in general, a far superior seed," Hoffman explains.[1] Around the same time, Dr. Mehmet Oz started promoting chia as a "superfood" on the *Oprah Winfrey Show*. He showed fans how to incorporate chia into their diets by adding it to smoothies and muffins.[2]

Chia, Hoffman discovered, has a long history; for example, Mayan warriors consumed it as early as 3,000 BC, and it was revered for its energy content and healing powers. Chia's nutritional profile indicated that it is the ultimate health food: it not only features omega-3s and antioxidants but also has balanced dietary fiber and minerals and is a complete protein. Hoffman noticed that she found an increase in her energy after adding chia seeds to her daily diet, and began using them in everything. "Cookies, bread, beverages, you name it and I put chia seeds in it," she recalls.[3] "It became a huge hit with my family and my friends. If someone was having a party and I asked what I could bring, they immediately requested one of my chia items—people couldn't get enough of them."

So she decided that she would start a food and beverage company that was built upon the chia seed. Obviously, this was a tremendous undertaking, but Hoffman describes herself as "A tenacious soul, full of passion . . . I didn't know anything about the food industry—absolutely nothing. But what I did know was that I wanted to be of service. I wanted to serve humanity and the planet. And I wanted to do that with chia seeds because I truly feel that they are magical."

She wanted to create a company that would "seed the soul." According to the Mamma Chia website, Hoffman's objective would be to connect her chia products to the user's soul, and her company's mission would be to share the magic of chia and lead in its renaissance.

After meeting Odwalla founder Greg Steltenpohl and receiving his advice, Hoffman decided to start with beverages. Her chia beverage, with its focus on the seeds, would be anything but your standard juice beverage—and it would not be ground-up seeds mixed in with a smoothie concoction. Instead, the chia seeds would be whole, and *suspended* in the beverage. Hoffman had a strong vision for the product: "The chia seed is all about vitality. If we were going to share the magic of chia seeds, then we needed the seeds themselves to make that happen. The seed—and the entire seed—had to be an essential part of product."

After a few operational hiccups, her production team was able to create the envisioned beverage. The product line launched with four different fruit flavors with names like Blackberry Hibiscus, Raspberry Passion, and Coconut Mango. True to Hoffman's vision, the seeds were suspended in the beverage, which had the texture of Jell-O. It was a drink to be savored, not swallowed in great gulps.

She would call it Mamma Chia. As Hoffman explains, "Well, first [the name] just has a nice ring to it. But more importantly, we were looking for a conscious connection with our consumers. We were looking to combine the idea of mother earth, the divine earth and its soul, with an honest and uplifting personality. The name connoted feeding your soul—which was what we wanted to do. We wanted to create a movement—a movement around chia."

That hoped-for movement was summarized by three lines on the label:

- Fun for Your Mouth—Great for Your Body!
- Seed Your Soul
- Seed Your Community

Each message represented an aspect of the brand that Hoffman hoped would ultimately connect with the consumer. Mamma Chia's Jell-O-like texture, floating chia seeds, and innovative flavors resulted in a product experience that proved that health could be fun. "Seed your soul" spoke to the energy in chia seeds and their potential to connect with the influencer on the most personal of levels—not just body, but soul too. And as an example of seeding a healthy, soulful community, Mamma Chia would donate 1 percent of sales to support local food systems.

Once the envisioned product was in production, the difficult work would begin. How would the Mamma Chia team get a consumer base, which had specific rules about what should and shouldn't be in a beverage, to even try this one? There were real mental barriers that had to be broken down. Beverages were perceived as smooth, drinkable, and thirst quenching. They were not perceived as having seeds floating in a concoction with the consistency of Jell-O. Hoffman truly believed that if the team could just get influencers to try the brand, they would be transformed by the "soulfulness" of chia seeds and would fall in love. Noting that consumers who were educated about the power of chia seeds would most likely shop at natural health food stores, she decided to call on Whole Foods. Armed with bottles of Mamma Chia, she went to the Whole Foods Southern Pacific regional offices, hoping that the product would sell itself to the regional buyer.

She says, "My plan was to convince Whole Foods to let me try it in a few stores. But the buyer took one look at the beverage and said, 'No I want you in all forty stores in the Southern Pacific region—it's exactly what my customers want.'" But the buyer also cautioned that it would be incredibly important to educate and establish the soulful connection with her potential customers that Hoffman was describing; otherwise the brand would be collecting dust on the shelf.

In response, Janie Hoffman personally went and set up tables inside the region's Whole Foods stores. As she encountered shoppers, she would simply ask, "Would you like to try Mamma Chia?" as she poured out the product. The passersby saw a gelatinous beverage with seeds floating in it and gave Hoffman looks that ranged from trepidation to discomfort to interest. When a shopper showed interest, Hoffman enthusiastically told the story of the magnificent chia seed, why it was important, what it meant to her, and how it could add meaning to the shopper's life. Quite often, what she found was an accepting consumer who "got it" and who was eager to experience this odd product with the weird texture. Customers who did try it found not just something healthy but also something great tasting and fun. According to Hoffman, the product sold itself. Mamma Chia engaged all five senses. From the sight of the seeds floating in the liquid to the thick texture, this experience, combined with the nutrient density of chia seeds, set a foundation for the project's relationship with these first influencers.

The fact that all this was taking place in Whole Foods was all to the better. Whole Foods was the ideal setting for a meeting between Mamma Chia and its potential influencers. The brands aligned perfectly—something the Whole Foods regional buyer had seen at a glance. At its core, Whole Foods is about enhancing the quality of one's life through education around health and wellness and purchasing the highest-quality natural and organic products. Enabling Mamma Chia to sample product to its consumer base was an implied endorsement from an extremely strong brand in that space.

The intimate connection that started with an impassioned Hoffman sampling the product by herself at individual Whole Food stores has now evolved. Mamma Chia has developed a group of "Word of Mouth Ambassadors" whose objective is to connect with consumers in a meaningful way. We'll talk about the idea of word of mouth in earnest later on, but it's worth noting here that the ambassadors Hoffman has recruited are sincerely committed to spreading the magic behind Mamma Chia. Hoffman says, "They do a better job of telling the story than I ever did." Although she spends significant time training, supporting, and coaching her ambassadors so that the message stays consistent wherever Mamma Chia is sampled, Hoffman still spends much of her time personally going out and evangelizing the Mamma Chia gospel. Of course, she is now a bit of a celebrity, and when Mamma Chia fans discover who she is, they aren't afraid to express their appreciation. She adds,

"Consumers come up to me and share all this joy and gratitude for providing them a brand that offers love and nutrition." According to Hoffman, that is what the success of her brand-consumer relationship comes down to: "I truly believe we are different from other brands because Mamma Chia is made with so much love. You can taste all the love that goes into our product."

EDUCATION IS KEY

A few lessons emerge from Mamma Chia's successful introduction that should be taken to heart. First, know that the initial meeting must *educate* the influencer as well as intrigue and entice—especially if your brand is radically different from what is commonly expected. If Mamma Chia had been sitting on a shelf with no sampling—no soulful story and no education—you can bet it would be collecting dust. It was a strange and different product. Hoffman and the Mamma Chia team had to make sure that they educated the consumers so as to coax them past any automatic resistance they might have. Almost always, without some type of education, consumers reject what is strange or different from their expectations. In his classic book *Blink*, Malcolm Gladwell shows how the Herman Miller office chair was rejected in consumer testing, yet became a huge success.[4] Executive office chairs weren't supposed to have netting for the backs; they were supposed to be made of leather. If initial consumer testing results had been followed, the chair would not have seen the light of day. But the team committed to conducting the necessary consumer education, and the brand succeeded.

It was also very important that Mamma Chia established a level of intimacy with the influencer. Think about it from a user standpoint. You are meeting the brand for the first time. You are in a location that puts you in the right frame of mind. You are then introduced to the brand by the founder of the business, who personally tells you the story of chia seeds, the origins of the brand, and how it helped her health and her soul, and who hands you a sample. How much more intimate can an educational experience get? This simple but intimate interaction enables Hoffman (or one of her ambassadors) to educate the consumer on the functional, emotional, and social benefits of Mamma Chia. It isn't a flashy marketing sampling program with glitz and glitter, but a simple one in which an intimate story and experience form the start of a relationship.

Some may feel that a brand may get too personal and risk alienating consumers. However, if up to this point you've done your job right and correctly identified your consumers' type and what they desire, you should know what they will best respond to. The Mamma Chia consumer is willing—even eager—to get to this level of intimacy. Recall, the right consumer to romance is someone who is willing to invest in your brand beyond the physical level (of functional benefits) and influence others to do the same. Mamma Chia makes no bones about its desire for a close connection. The message on the product label aligns with the brand's essence: Seed Your Soul. That is not superficial or manipulative: the brand seeks to connect immediately with the influencer; by introducing itself in a very nonthreatening, nonflashy, genuine way and through personalized storytelling, it accomplishes this goal.

MAKE IT MEMORABLE

Clearly, all brands aren't going to be able to achieve as intimate or educational an introduction as Mamma Chia, and many shouldn't. (The approach would have been all wrong for, say, Powerade.) But if you think about your brand, you will undoubtedly realize that there are users out there who are willing to embrace the brand beyond a surface-level meeting. Maybe it is at the emotional level. Maybe it is at the social level. Or maybe, in the case of Mamma Chia, it is at a soulful level. The point is to ensure that, regardless of the dynamics of a specific brand and category, the first meeting is a memorable one. Encounters that are crafted to be memorable—that enable a brand to showcase its best features in the most appealing light and to tell its story and educate—have a much better chance of sticking with potential users than random meetings. This is always the case, but is especially critical if the product stretches category expectations or otherwise has the potential to be perceived as "strange." The first meeting doesn't have to be a quick "Hi, nice to meet you, see you around" interaction. It may be better if it is a prolonged, memorable, and, if applicable, intimate conversation—as long as it's with the right consumer.

Mamma Chia quickly made inroads into a crowded beverage market; in fact, Hoffman was named BevNet's 2012 Person of the Year for her creation of "an entirely new category."[5] The brand has now expanded its distribution beyond natural foods outlets into mainstream grocery stores and plans to expand into additional food-based categories in the future. Hoffman continues to associate herself with chia seeds, publishing both a lifestyle book promoting their benefits as well as a cookbook in which all the recipes contain generous amounts of chia. Both Hoffman and her company's goals are aligned: communicate with a laserlike focus around the benefits of chia.

• • •

If we've done our job right and met that influencer under the right circumstances, then we have set the stage to grow the relationship further. The influencers will want to engage with our brand. After our initial meetings, our goal is to put the relationship on a trajectory that will serve to nurture and develop a growing bond. But it is also time to begin asking for something in return. A relationship, by definition, involves the interdependence of both parties. Up to now, we've not asked much of our consumer beyond his or her being receptive to our requests for connection. Once that connection is made, the dynamics can begin to change. As we saw in some of the stories in this chapter, the discussions that consumers have about our brand—their word of mouth—will be essential in taking the brand's relationship with both them and others to the next level. Chapter Five will explore the powerful concept of generating word of mouth.

5

MAKE IT MUTUAL

Which would you think has a better chance of succeeding over the long haul: a relationship in which the couple meets randomly in a bar, or a relationship in which the couple is introduced by a third party who knows both of them well enough to think that they may click with one another? With the random meeting, you are relying on yourself and your ability to immediately determine whether or not the person has potential for you. With the blind date, you are putting your faith in the friend who is setting you up. Not only does the friend know you and have some sense (more or less insightful) about what you want in a partner, but you will probably make more of an effort to give the "setup" a chance, because the friend has gone to the effort. Now think about this kind of dynamic as it relates to brands and consumers.

Stuart Sheldon would argue that the "setup" or recommendation from a respected source has a much better chance of long-term success than a random brand "meeting." Stu's professional cause is to educate others to the power of word of mouth (WOM) and to help his clients embrace word-of-mouth marketing (WOMM) as both a strategy and tactic in their businesses.

Sheldon has plenty of experience on the topic. His first foray into WOM and WOMM came in 2003, as senior brand manager for Coca-Cola in the United States, where he launched the first 100 percent WOMM program in the history of The Coca-Cola Company. Sheldon remembers, "Our results were so strong, so positive, the analytics team had to triple-check for accuracy." Two years later, Coca-Cola assigned him to head a cross-functional team that explored how Coca-Cola should integrate WOM and WOMM into its business.

Currently, as president of Escalate, an experiential and WOMM agency, Sheldon will convince you that there is no more powerful way to increase the chances of success of a brand-consumer relationship. Of course, WOMM is nothing new. It is the idea of tapping into our influencer's network of friends, relatives, and coworkers so as to share a message with the appropriate members of that network. These folks then pass along the message to their expanded networks. If an influencer has a positive experience with a brand, he or she will pass it on to friends, family members, or acquaintances who, due to their relationship with the original consumer, will seriously consider the recommendation. As the message gets passed along, it becomes diluted and must continually be reinforced by traditional brand communication so that this network effect can be maintained. When it works, it's like a chain of arranged blind dates that go well and add up to many, many strong brand-consumer relationships.

Sheldon believes that marketers typically misuse or ignore this golden opportunity to join and benefit from the conversation around their brands. He stresses that WOMM involves a two-way conversation between brand and consumer. "Word-of-mouth marketing is like being in a relationship. You're proving to your partner that you listen to them, you hear them, and respect their opinion. You might not do exactly what they request every time, but you do have to consistently demonstrate you value what they say."[1]

What Sheldon is pointing out is that brands and consumers should ultimately communicate as two people in a relationship would communicate with each other. Many brands (really the marketers behind them) try to pretend that they are the only ones in control of the relationship—which works about as well as it does in a relationship between two people. In that mode, if a brand screams loud enough (think large amounts of paid advertising or even millions who click "like" on Facebook), the marketing team might believe that they can get consumers to think, say, and do exactly what the marketing plan dictates. But in reality, consumers will generate their own direct opinions about a brand on the basis of a number of factors, including (and primarily) through their own experience. They will also not be shy in sharing those opinions with others—and every year there are more and more powerful outlets for this sharing. What consumers say is well beyond the control of the marketer. But it's not beyond our influence.

Sheldon says, "Consumer conversations happen constantly. Billions of times in the U.S. alone people are talking about my brand. The questions that I must ask myself are, (1) Do I want to know what consumers say about my brand? (2) If yes, what conversations do I want to join or start? And finally, (3) How do I do it?"

We'll assume that the answer to question 1 is yes. As Sheldon says, the conversation is already happening. "With hundreds of case studies, papers, and books that document WOM as the primary driver of perception, purchase, and perhaps even future performance of publicly traded companies," he explains, "the brand manager who cares about the long-term viability of their charge definitely answers yes to question 1."

The answers to questions 2 and 3 will determine the success of a WOMM strategy. If a brand's ultimate goal is to cultivate consumers who are passionate lifelong advocates—with a connection to the brand so strong that consumers want to shout about it from the rooftops—the advocates must be the right people. They must be the consumers whom the brand wants as its advocates. This is the classic influencer strategy that we've been discussing: the influencer must represent a personification of the brand and be someone whom others admire and want to follow. But there's more. In an ideal world, these influencers will themselves know the right people to influence.

Sheldon says, "If the influencer is talking to the wrong people about a brand, then the wrong consumer is getting the message, but more importantly that influencer begins to lose credibility. A healthy brand has an army of advocates knowledgeable enough about their own relationships with others to know with whom to share the brand message. It's the difference between successful and unsuccessful word-of-mouth programs."

According to WOMMA, the average adult is bombarded with three thousand branded messages a day. Three-quarters of those consumers say that they question the honesty of those brands who pay to put those messages on TV screens, radio stations, outdoor billboards, digital ad banners, and so on. At the same time, according to the Keller Fay Group, a WOMM measurement company, almost 80 percent of consumers indicate that WOM plays a role in their purchase, with some 20 percent indicating that their entire purchase decision was made through WOM. So how does a marketing team create a program that generates positive WOM? Let's look at one that was incredibly successful—coincidentally, one that Stu Sheldon helped create.

REAL COKE TASTE AND ZERO CALORIES

In 2005, The Coca-Cola Company embarked on the largest cola soft drink launch since New Coke was introduced in 1985. The company certainly hoped this one would go better. In an effort to keep calorie-conscious males within the Coca-Cola franchise, Coke was going to launch a new zero-calorie cola product. Although the company had a very successful diet cola product in Diet Coke, it lacked a no-calorie version that had a taste similar to the sugared version of Coca-Cola.

Market research showed that some consumers, predominantly male, wouldn't make the transition from Coca-Cola to

Diet Coke when they got older and more calorie conscious. This group of consumers wanted the trademark Coca-Cola taste but without the sugar and calories. Coke had thought it had discovered the secret to keeping these guys in the franchise a year earlier with a seventy-calorie cola named Coca-Cola C2, but C2 just wasn't what consumers were looking for.[2] They would choose either to sacrifice the taste for the benefit of no calories or to just have all the taste, calories be damned. They weren't going to halfway sacrifice taste and halfway sacrifice calories. Obviously, the ideal product would give them both benefits: a great taste and no calories. So Coke went back into the laboratory to develop a zero-calorie product that was closer to the sugared version of Coca-Cola than any other that had ever been introduced into the marketplace. The brand would be called Coca-Cola Zero. It would focus on young men seeking real cola taste with no calories—and Coke's goal would be for it to become huge.

The brand was launched with an ad called "Chill" that was a modernized version of the classic 1972 Coca-Cola ad, "I'd Like to Teach the World to Sing." Although the ad drove significant buzz, it emphasized refreshment. It didn't talk about taste. A new group director, Caren Pasquale Seckler, would change that. Her objective: to focus like a laser on the brand's Coca-Cola Classic–like taste, saying, "Everything we are doing is about communicating that [taste] message."[3]

Coca-Cola Zero launched a new tongue-in-cheek campaign that featured two Coca-Cola Classic "brand managers" (actors) who set up meetings with real-life attorneys (including real estate and immigration lawyers). The meetings were recorded with a hidden camera; the attorneys had no idea they were being filmed. The ads depicted the brand managers wanting to sue the Coke Zero brand team for "taste infringement"—Coke Zero tasted too much like Coke. The lawyers, not realizing that they were being set up, generally sat there flabbergasted, but tried their best to respond. The campaign was funny and memorable, and set high expectations for the product.

The campaign established a reputation that made potential users want to meet this new brand. The marketing team needed to get the product into consumers' hands in a way that was memorable. So they put out a brief that requested agencies to put together an experiential trial program. As part of their pitch, Sheldon and his agency, Escalate, recommended that WOM be a fundamental pillar of the program. Knowing that it was critical for their consumer relationship to quickly accelerate beyond meeting, Coke Zero selected Escalate as the agency for this program.

Passing It On

Traditional marketing wisdom said that the company needs to be the advocate of the brand, putting as many samples into the hands of consumers as possible, winning attention through ad buys, sponsorships, and other company-generated efforts. The Escalate model was radically different: in its plan, consumers would gain interest through the advocacy and recommendations of others—their peers. Sheldon put it in dating terms: "Traditional marketing is all about kissing as many girls as you possibly can as quickly as you can. We think the brand should spend the time to get to know someone first so that if you do kiss them, the odds of that kiss leading to more are dramatically higher."

This program wouldn't have that mass-produced, kiss-as-many-as-you-can feel. It wouldn't be created in the typical agency brainstorming session with brand input. Instead, it would be developed and executed with significant involvement of the self-named Coke Zero Connection (CZC). The CZC team would be recruited from the biggest initial fans of Coke Zero—the Coke Zero influencers, those young males between the ages of sixteen and twenty-four who were looking for real Coke taste, but without the calories. They would be invited to develop their best idea for a program that would get friends and family interested in and engaged with the brand.

The first step would be to create this community of ardent Coke Zero fans. Trying to locate the most fervent fans of a relatively new brand would be a challenge, but the Escalate team was up for it. Coke has a loyalty program for all its brands called My Coke Rewards, in which consumers are rewarded with points to purchase "stuff" anytime they purchase any Coke product—as long as they input the code on the bottom of the cap into their online account. This program gives Coke the benefit of knowing who each member is and what brands he or she buys, so the team was readily able to identify a group of frequent purchasers of Coke Zero.

To join the CZC, you also had to exhibit behavior that showed you could influence others, and you had to show that you were a huge fan of the brand. A process was developed to follow up directly with those consumers initially deemed to be potential influencers. On the basis of a number of factors, such as their age, location, frequency of Coke Zero purchases, and willingness to engage in marketing activities, some twelve hundred of the most active, engaged, and ardent Coke Zero fans were invited to join the team.[4]

Over the next eight months, the CZC community members would engage—both online and in person—in conversations and workshops with the Coke Zero brand team and its affiliated agencies. The discussions centered around what was important to them, their passion points, the sports and games they enjoyed, and what they did in their free time. They were also asked to identify the best place to hold experiential events in their local markets. All of these fed into the program design including the final name, Coke Zero "It's Possible," also developed by the CZC. The agency then refined and implemented the program, with continued involvement from the CZC through feedback forms and follow-up interviews.

As the CZC community was designing Coke Zero "It's Possible," something interesting started to happen: CZC community members started talking about it. Almost 70 percent of them indicated that their likelihood of sharing information about Coke Zero with others went up. In fact, tens of thousands of conversations about Coke Zero were taking place—in person, on the phone, and online—that wouldn't have been happening if the CZC community hadn't been engaged. Furthermore, some 45 percent of the CZC members indicated that they got their friends to try Coke Zero for the first time. All this was before the trial portion of the program even started!

Driving the Talk

The Coke Zero experience became a traveling interactive event found at various live venues, from concerts to sporting events. The goal would be to deliver some fifteen million samples of Coke Zero. It launched on New Year's Day 2009 at the Rose Bowl in Los Angeles, and over the next twelve months would reach two thousand events in forty markets. In part a result of CZC's recommendations, activation partners included the NCAA, AMC Theaters, Disney, Six Flags, and Papa John's, among others. Components included a gaming lounge featuring EA Sports and Xbox games as well as traditional arcade-type games (think basketball shooting games). The all-important WOM measure would be tracked: guests were asked to participate in a custom research project enabling them to tell the brand about the conversations they were having about Coke Zero. Through this measure, the Coke Zero team discovered that of those who tried Coke Zero for the first time at the event, some 78 percent reported that they recommended it to an average of eleven others. But even more powerful, the brand saw a tremendous increase in the number of consumers who had already "met" the brand before and were engaging with it again. Over two-thirds of those who had already tried the product and participated in the experience intended to recommend the brand to others.

But what was truly noteworthy about the program was what was being said. Research showed that the value went way beyond the experiences themselves. Two items were measured. The first was the direct number of individuals impacted. Three groups were measured: Generation Zero (G0, those in direct contact with Coke Zero at an event), Generation One (G1, friends and acquaintances who were told something about the event by G0), and Generation Two (G2, friends and acquaintances of G1, representing the secondary pass-along rate). The second measure was of the quality of the conversations. In other words, the researchers didn't just note whether a conversation occurred; they also monitored what was being said. And what they found was remarkable.

Let's start with the quality of the conversations. Of the conversations that occurred between those who went to the event and their friends and family (G0 and G1), 58 percent were about the Coke Zero taste, and 23 percent were about the brand's zero calories. In other words, over 80 percent of the measured conversations that were taking place about Coca-Cola Zero were exactly what the brand team wanted the message to be. That was huge!

Of those who experienced the event (G0), almost 80 percent indicated that they told at least one other person about it. When it was all calculated out, G0 told some forty million people (G1). As those forty million people heard about it, they also told others in their network (G2). Although the WOM effects weren't as powerful as with G0, quite a few members of G1 shared the message with at least one person. The Coke Zero team estimated that G2 exceeded seventy million people. All told, the total number of people who heard about the event exceeded 110 million people!

A thought-provoking aspect of the program was this: the live on-site experience generated not just a stronger pass-along rate but also communicated the right message more frequently than social media conversation (sometimes referred to as "digiWOMM") about Coke Zero. How much more frequently was the right Coke Zero message (real Coke taste, zero calories) passed along by those who actually experienced the event versus those who heard of Coke Zero through social media? Based on what we've discussed, what would be your guess? You can probably assume that consumers who experienced the actual event got the message more clearly and were more likely to tell others about it. But how much more did they pass along the right message? Was it 20 percent more? 50 percent more? 100 percent more? Guess again. The pass-along rate with the proper message was *fifteen times* higher if a consumer attended a live event than if one had just interacted via social media. In other words, it proved to be much more difficult to accurately communicate the brand message to others if one had engaged only digitally and had not actually engaged in the experience.

Wait a second, you say. All we've heard about for the past few years is how social media is changing the way we need to market. Isn't it all about spreading a message digitally and engaging with the consumer in an electronic medium? Well, sure, but only to an extent. Social media cannot and will not ever replace the actual brand experience. Because this is a point that many marketers may be forgetting right now (or that they just don't understand), let's spend some time talking about how this is so.

SOCIAL MEDIA IN THE GRAND SCHEME OF THINGS

The WOMM measurement firm Keller Fay has a syndicated service known as TalkTrack, which measures active WOM.

Think of it as the equivalent of a Nielsen TV measuring system, except that it measures the brand discussions among individuals any way that they occur. Included are online conversations and social media sharing as well as the more traditional person-to-person conversations, such as telephone and face-to-face discussions. TalkTrack interviews a large, nationally representative sample (each year, thirty-six thousand Americans thirteen years of age and older) and measures some 350,000 conversations about brands annually, updating each twenty-four-hour period.

According to TalkTrack, the amount of social sharing that takes place offline, primarily in a face-to-face or phone (speaking, not texting) context, dwarfs anything online. Even though our perception is that we are a society addicted to our smartphones and iPads, the fact is that most of our conversations about brands take place in the physical presence of someone else. According to TalkTrack, offline WOM is responsible for 90 percent of all brand-related WOM, whereas social media represents 2 percent.

Even within the online space, social media doesn't dominate the conversations. Ed Keller, president of Keller Fay, states, "When it comes to online word of mouth around brands, IM or texting accounts for the greatest share, about half of the conversations. E-mail and social media are about half that level, so IM/texting and e-mail account for more than three quarters of all online brand conversations while social media accounts for a quarter."[5]

These finding are consistent with that of Alexis Madrigal, who in an article in the *Atlantic* in October 2012, revealed an analysis which indicated that when users are referred to other websites, most of it doesn't come from social media. In fact, Madrigal reported that some 69 percent of Web traffic came through "unmeasured ways," usually in the form of emails and texts, compared to only 20 percent coming from Facebook and 6 percent coming from Twitter.[6]

There is a common saying in the business world: "You move what you measure." As marketers, we tend to get hung up on the latest craze—whether it's Facebook or Pinterest or the hot new social media site—and naturally want to ensure that our brands are present in these locations. Academics and analytics firms are busily trying to put the proper measuring devices around this new technology. Cutting edge and innovative technology will certainly continue to grow, and we are only just beginning to understand its power. Though as of now, in the grand scheme of things, it's miniscule.

Having an effective relationship with another human being still requires face-to-face interactions. The same can be said of brands. When Ed Keller states, "Just because WOM is difficult to measure, doesn't mean it's not real, or that marketers should ignore it."[7]

If anything, Keller's data show that we should be paying more attention to the actual brand-consumer interaction. The marketers who ignore reality, and only emphasize digital interactions at the expense of real consumer experiences, will risk building an artificial relationship with the consumer. People live real lives. As marketers, we must find ways to tap into those real lives and discover how we can establish a brand romance by sharing experiences. Seeing through the social media hype can give us pause to determine whether or not we are, in fact, doing the right things to connect more holistically to our consumer and ensure that our relationship is heading to the next level.

CRAFTING THE IDEAL EXPERIENCE

How can we develop an experience that enables us to proactively engage consumers in conversations with others? Our relationship must be at a point where consumers want to tell others about their romance with the brand. Based on what we've discussed so far in this chapter, there are three mantras to keep in mind: leverage your evangelists, emphasize the interaction, and understand the proper role of social media.

Leverage Your Evangelists

Every brand success story we've analyzed so far has identified a core group of consumers who are the most ardent, fervent users of that brand. The big athletes on high school campuses with Powerade; the upscale, trendsetting young women for smartwater; those interesting twenty-somethings for Dos Equis—all were influencers who played a crucial role in initially becoming brand adopters and spreading the message. But what we saw with Coca-Cola Zero was that the marketing team didn't just rely on passive influencer communication; they proactively encouraged the influencers to become brand evangelists through a WOMM program.

The Coke Zero team gave their brand evangelists the ultimate responsibility. They had them play a major role in the creation of a significant brand marketing program. This gave the evangelists not only ownership in the success of the brand but also a platform to discuss this new brand with their friends. Because the CZC members were an attractive, influential group, the fact that they were discussing the program before it had even launched gave Coca-Cola Zero the right buzz among the right people. The program was successful before it even started. How might you leverage your biggest evangelists not just to talk about your brand but to play an active role in recruiting others?

Emphasize the Interaction

In the grand scheme of consumer behavior, it is relatively easy to stimulate awareness and consumer trial of your product—just put enough resources and money behind your effort. It is less easy to get someone to return to your brand. As we've discussed, grounding your initial reputation and ensuring that the first experiences a consumer has with the brand are as wonderful as they can be will take you a long way toward success.

At Coca-Cola, we always looked closely at the repeat number—the measure that indicated whether a consumer actually came back to the brand a second, third, and fourth time. That was when you knew that this budding relationship had the potential to turn into a romance—and whether the potential existed to recruit enough early evangelists to begin a brand movement. Although television and radio spots, online videos, and social media postings play a role, it all has to start with that "face-to-brand" experience.

The first few experiences that the consumer has with the brand, as demonstrated in many of our examples, are absolutely critical in determining how the overall brand-consumer relationship will manifest itself. Recall Mamma Chia,

Coca-Cola Zero, and Powerade. The brands that invest in the initial experiences, ensuring that they are tied into consumer needs and desires, are the ones that tend to be successful. These initial experiences determine two things: (1) the impact that the brand will have beyond the initial trial-and-repeat stage and (2) whether the impact will be felt strongly enough that the consumers will want to spread the message to those near and dear to them. At this point, we are in a position to ask the consumers to take some risks and put themselves out there for the brand. If the initial experiences and first few "dates" are meaningful enough, consumers will feel strong enough about the brand not only to engage more with it but also to share those feelings with others.

Therefore, the quality of the brand-consumer experience is far more important than the quantity of experiences. A key principle of effective WOMM is that you are better off with fewer consumers having a better brand experience. Why? As we have seen, the pass-along factor will be higher. I'd rather have half as many consumers engage in a great experience (as opposed to a mediocre one) if they have a pass-along rate that is three times higher than that of the consumers having an inferior experience. This doesn't even reflect the higher percentage of the "right" message being passed along. We can create the best ads, social media messages, and viral videos, but at the end of the day, the consumer is more likely to share a positive real-life experience.

Understand the Role of Social Media

Although, as we've seen, social media pales in comparison to the actual product experience in its contribution to growing the relationship, that is not to say that it isn't important. In fact, in Chapters Six and Seven, I will showcase viral programs in which social media played a significant role by augmenting other marketing initiatives to help spread the early word. But we have to understand how best to use it.

Take the Coca-Cola Zero example we just reviewed. Most brands don't have a well-maintained loyalty database to source their biggest fans, as Coke Zero was able to do with the My Coke Rewards stable of consumers. But marketers *can* use social media to gain new access to consumers. As consumers, we share a lot of personal information about ourselves via social media sites, frequent shopper and rewards cards, and online ordering. When we share information, it changes not only our relationship with other people but also our relationship with brands. This is where "big data," which for our purposes can be defined as a collection of key pieces of consumer information grouped together so that it creates a large data set, comes in. It's changing the way marketers learn about consumers.

John "JD" Doughney is a client partner at Facebook. He consults some of the biggest brands in the world to ensure that they are fully leveraging Facebook to drive impact for their business. He will tell you that the information that we as consumers willingly provide marketers can determine whether or not we are a good match in a relationship setting.[8] That same information can also help us as marketers in determining who our potential brand evangelists are and how we can best communicate with them. Consumers' actions in the social media space tell a lot about them, their interests, and what they might have in common with a brand. For instance, they "like" things, they become "fans" of pages, they comment on things, and they even share things with their friends. Social platforms can give marketers insights into how potential consumers view the world. But as was crystal clear in the Dos Equis example, it undoubtedly will take more than just social media to understand your consumer in a *deeper* way. Bottom line: it is one tool (albeit a powerful one) that should be part of a larger strategy.

Doughney says, "Marketers should design programs around people, not technology. Brands don't need to have a Facebook strategy or a Twitter strategy. They need to have a marketing strategy that is mapped to business objectives."

This brings us back to my earlier analogy of the six-year-old softball players (everyone chasing the ball and no one covering first base). In our rush to be "technology savvy," we are losing the bigger strategic picture. We are forgetting about the consumer, thinking that if we have the right social media plan in place, we are guaranteed success. Doughney adds, "A social media plan is an 'and,' not an 'or.' As marketers, we need to think about it as a way to engage in more ongoing conversations with consumers." He will tell you that when marketers think that two or three consumer communication campaigns over the course of a calendar year will be enough, it's the equivalent of buying one's significant other an anniversary gift, birthday gift, and Valentine's gift and ignoring him or her the rest of the year. In most of our relationships, it's the little day-to-day interactions that help grow the relationship and make it stronger. Marketers should think about how they can weave together their larger campaigns with lighter interactions that happen more frequently. Doughney adds, "This works well on social platforms like Facebook because it is another place where people communicate with one another. Brands, likewise, can communicate with more precision in the social space."

This is where social media will play a role. Although I believe that its talk value will pale in comparison to that of the more intimate brand-consumer interactions, social media is absolutely necessary not just for maintaining a dialogue but for creating ongoing conversations around commonalities that the consumer and the brand may have. It can be an important part of the marketing mix to augment those brand experiences by connecting with the people who matter most to the brand, its self-described fans.

Doughney says, "Social media enables us to customize our messaging so that the consumer truly feels like it is for them." He notes that marketers have traditionally looked at messaging with no idea of where their relationship with a consumer stands or where it has been in the past. He adds, "Instead of saying, 'Hi! Nice to meet you! Let's go on a European vacation together!' social media may help the marketing team in knowing which consumer is ready for such a big step."

He's right. Traditionally, the message that marketers would send to consumers had no bearing on where they were in the evolution of the relationship. Social media has the potential to let the brand communicate with the consumer on a one-to-one basis that aligns better with where the relationship stands. In other words, social media can enable marketers to personalize the brand's communication more often.

• • •

We've connected so well with our consumer base that they are now talking about us with others. The romance is continuing to progress. At some point, both parties need to ask themselves, "Is it time to make a commitment?" How will we know? In the next chapter, we'll find out that answer.

6

DEEPEN THE CONNECTION

The highlight of my family's summer vacation wasn't the historic sites like Independence Hall in Philadelphia or Fort McHenry in Baltimore. Rather, for my wife, our ten-year-old son, and our twin six-year-old daughters, the high point of the trip was something that we tacked on at the very end, something that required us to drive some two hours west of Philadelphia into the farm country of central Pennsylvania to the little town of Hershey. I'm talking about Hershey's Chocolate World.

As I walked from the parking lot into the building, my immediate reaction was to notice how many cars were there. It was a random Monday, and the place was quite full. A long ticket line ran around the corner; people were waiting to pay up to $40 per person to experience an array of Hershey-branded experiences. This was not the Hershey amusement park, which was across the street and required a separate ticket. Rather, Hershey's Chocolate World would immerse its visitors in the famous candy bar brand. Exhibits included a ride that depicted how chocolate bars were made, a trolley tour of the facility's grounds, a "4D" movie experience, a course on how to taste chocolate, and a hands-on exhibit that allowed guests to create their own candy bar.

As my son and his sisters put on their aprons and placed the netting around their heads, then ran excitedly into the area where they would choose the ingredients, customize their label, and even watch their candy bar being produced, I witnessed how the Hershey brand was coming to life for every visitor. Hershey's candy-bar-making experience was putting an indelible imprint on the memories of my children, much as it had done to me some thirty years ago when I visited the factory as a child. Many visitors would be there for a few days, experiencing Chocolate World one day and Hershey Park the next. They hadn't just driven for miles; they were willing to fork out their hard-earned dollars to essentially be marketed to in a unique way, soaking up everything Hershey. I am also sure that most visited the Hershey store—bigger than most grocery stores—and bought up a myriad of Hershey-branded clothing, household goods, and furniture items, as well as recently produced Hershey candy.

Hershey is not the only brand to have developed a popular consumer experience that links its brand in an amusement park or entertainment setting. There are six LEGOLAND parks throughout the world, with three more under construction. In addition, ten LEGOLAND Discovery Centers—a smaller indoor family LEGO entertainment center—are found worldwide. According to the LEGOLAND website, the largest LEGO parks draw over 1.5 million visitors per year. All the parks have one goal: to enable consumers to experience the LEGO brand through rides, education, and creative interaction.

Hershey and LEGOLAND represent a phenomenon: brand-oriented amusement parks and dedicated brand tours are popping up everywhere. The World of Coca-Cola, Coors Golden Brewery tour, the Ben and Jerry's tour, the CNN tour, Crayola Experience, and Kellogg Cereal City, to name a few, all offer unique experiences to visitors while manifesting the brand in appealing ways. These interactive experiences offer yet another means of deepening the connection between brand and consumer. When consumers are going out of their way and paying money to experience your brand's messaging beyond the traditional thirty-second ad, you know that the romance is strong. Of course, not all brands can customize and create amusement parks and factory tours. That does not mean that brands can't do things to make the romance special and continue to "court" the consumer. Even mature brands must work to find new ways to surprise and delight their user base.

In this chapter, we'll focus on the ways that brands can deepen their connection with consumers. Many of the ideas build on what originally brought the brand and consumer together, explored on a different level. As is true of any relationship, a brand can't ignore the consumer once he or she is committed. The marketing team must continue to reinforce the philosophy that the consumer is special.

MAKING THE CONSUMER FEEL IMPORTANT

On May 31, 2010, a select few fans waited outside their favorite quick-service restaurant for an exclusive privilege. They were participating in the most anticipated sandwich launch by this brand in over twenty years. In fact, they would be among the first people in the world to try Chick-fil-A's new Spicy Chicken Sandwich—and they were there by personal invitation. Why had these particular people been given this opportunity?

Just ten days earlier, thousands of Chick-fil-A e-club members received an invitation to visit a special website to make a reservation, yes a *reservation*, to try the Spicy Chicken Sandwich sometime between May 31 and June 5. Starting on June 7, the sandwich would officially be available to the general public. (June 6 was a Sunday, and Chick-fil-A is famously closed on Sundays.) Chick-fil-A e-club members had to reserve a personalized time and a store location to try this new product. Once consumers made a reservation, two things happened: (1) they were required to print out the official invitation, and (2) they were given the option of announcing their reservation on Facebook and Twitter and recommending the reservation site to a friend. To try the Spicy Chicken Sandwich, they had to take the official invitation in their name to the selected Chick-fil-A store during the designated time. The employees at the store actually checked their ID before giving the sandwich to them. If they didn't have a reservation, they wouldn't be allowed to try it. Chick-fil-A wouldn't even let them pay for one. The sandwich was strictly off-limits to anyone who hadn't made a reservation ahead of time and brought in both his invitation and his identification.

This was a unique sampling program. "We are especially excited about the reservation-based sampling of our new sandwich with our loyal customers," William F. "Woody" Faulk, Chick-fil-A vice president of brand strategy and design, said. "We want to invite our customers to taste the flavor and quality of this spicy sandwich, but we don't want a cattle-call setting where we won't be able to extend 'second mile' service to our customers. This reservation system provides a more personalized way to introduce our exciting menu addition."[1]

The perceived exclusivity of this innovative sampling program generated a significant upside not just for the new product but for the Chick-fil-A brand as a whole. Think about that for a moment. We aren't talking about a new brand. We're talking about a strongly entrenched brand with a very dedicated consumer base. For years, Chick-fil-A's high service standards had made consumers feel important when dining in their restaurants. Now they were making consumers feel even more special in the way the sampling program was implemented.

We first discussed the concept of specialness in the context of introducing a new brand, Powerade, to a new user, but the principle applies here as well. If you want your relationship to survive, you don't just turn off the charm once you've got the guy or girl. You keep at it. By giving its e-club members "first dibs" on trying the new sandwich, Chick-fil-A was telling them they were important. Consequently, Chick-fil-A fans quickly gobbled up the reservations so that they could be the first to try the highly anticipated sandwich and share their thoughts with friends and acquaintances.

As I mentioned, the conventional wisdom is that as a marketer, you want to get your product in the hands of as many people as you possibly can. When I was a brand manager, sampling agencies would pitch us by telling us that if we paid them X dollars, they would be able to deliver Y million samples of products. It was all about quantity. As various facets of the Mamma Chia, smartwater, and Chick-fil-A stories show, that may not be the way to go if you want to have a real consumer relationship.

Although I am sure Chick-fil-A wanted to get the sandwich into many customer hands (and ultimately did), it made a conscious decision to create a special experience. The experience mattered much more than the absolute number. The company wasn't just going to randomly throw chicken sandwiches at every customer the minute he or she walked in the door, with a "Try Me!" message flashing like a neon sign on the Las Vegas strip. Chick-fil-A was telling the consumer that he or she wasn't just a number. The consumer was *invited* to sample the product.

Think about that word for a minute: invitation. An invitation is defined as a courteous or complimentary way of requesting someone's presence or participation. That doesn't bear much resemblance to restaurant employees in a mall food court handing out chicken bites on toothpicks to lines of people. Not everybody was going to be able to try the new Spicy Chicken Sandwich, so it had an aura of scarcity associated with it.

Chick-fil-A was employing some of the WOMM practices that we examined in connection with the launch of a new brand. Its unique reservation system enabled e-club members not just to make a reservation but also to announce to their friends and family online that they were going to try the new sandwich. Also important is that members could invite friends to make a reservation to try the sandwich. Chick-fil-A was giving them the opportunity to be evangelists for a product they *hadn't even tried*. The e-club members were more than happy to oblige. Why? First, Chick-fil-A had chosen *them*. Much like Powerade and smartwater, Chick-fil-A had a loyal following of fans who were pleased to have been selected to share the good news that there was a new product coming. It didn't matter that they hadn't tried it. They had enough faith in the Chick-fil-A brand to recommend this new sandwich to others. Chick-fil-A made it easy for them to do so. It was classic WOMM, bringing together both sides of the relationship in a seamless and mutually beneficial exchange.

In fact, the innovative reservation system created a huge buzz around the brand and the sandwich, resulting in more than 150 broadcast mentions and placements in media outlets.[2] As a result, Chick-fil-A had thousands of fans sharing the news that there was a new sandwich available and that you had to make a reservation to try it. In this case, social media was the appropriate tool, and showed its power. The perception of scarcity continued while thousands and thousands of consumers, driven by an ever-increasing media buzz around a sandwich that required advance planning, made online reservations to try it. The scarcity factor was *all* perception, of course—there were plenty of the sandwiches for all. Yet every influencer who received one felt special—and this specialness cascaded onto the brand.

The company gave away 1.2 million sandwiches during the one-week sampling period. The following two weeks, they sold 3.3 million.[3] All told, Chick-fil-A sold more than 58 million Spicy Chicken Sandwiches during the last half of 2010, which averages as 110 sandwiches per minute or almost 2 per second.[4]

A "BRAND FOR ME"

Consider the following twenty-two brands that range across the entertainment, technology, sports, consumer packaged goods, and automobile sectors, among others:

- Harley-Davidson
- Coca-Cola
- Starbucks
- BMW
- Lifetime
- Amazon
- *Mad Men*
- HBO
- Apple
- Boston Red Sox
- Sony
- Nike
- Walt Disney
- Turner Classic Movies
- NFL
- AMC
- Tide
- ABC
- Target
- *The Simpsons*
- NASCAR
- Pottery Barn

Let's say that we gather together a group of consumers to understand their "fanship" for each of these brands, the ones who we believe are truly in love with them. Some of these groups might be larger than others based on the sheer size of the brand, of course. A group of passionate Disney fans is probably going to be larger than that of *Mad Men*. But we're not thinking about absolute size in numbers right now. We're thinking about how passionate each group is toward an individual brand. Now let's say we ask them all how much they agreed with this statement: "I feel like this brand was created with me in mind." Which one of the twenty-two brands listed do you think would rank highest?

Before you answer, think about the question itself: "I feel like this brand was created with me in mind." Why do you think we are looking specifically at that question? For a consumer to agree with that statement, he or she must feel very connected with the brand. It's pretty powerful stuff. This resembles the point in a relationship where the parties truly believe that they were made for each other. When they've hit that stage, it is a major milestone. They're not thinking about the next date, the next week, or the next month. They're thinking about a lifetime together.

So, returning to the question of which brand's fans feel most strongly that the brand was truly created for them, if you said Apple, you'd be right. But that probably isn't too surprising. Apple has done a remarkable job of building strong passion among its users and creating a brand that its biggest fans truly feel was created for their specific needs. But who is number two? Disney? The NFL? NASCAR? Nike? Harley-Davidson? Coca-Cola? All these brands have extremely passionate consumer bases. But in the study, none of them ranked in second place.

What did finish right behind Apple on this key question? Believe it or not, it was Turner Classic Movies (TCM). I'm betting that you're probably really surprised right now—that is, unless you're a TCM fan. But if you aren't, you may be sitting there thinking to yourself, *Turner Classic Movies? Why? How?*

One person who wasn't surprised at all was Jeff Gregor, chief marketing officer of Turner Networks, including TNT and TBS, and the general manager of TCM. Gregor explains the basis of the brand this way: "TCM has been able to create a true love affair with our consumer base. We aren't just a classic movie channel. We show movies the way movies are supposed to be seen. That has been our mission from day 1."[5]

A Unique Proposition

Before we dig deeper into what makes TCM unique and so well loved by its biggest fans, let's look at the business itself. TCM has a unique business model. The network is now twenty years old, and although it is one of Turner's smallest in terms of revenue, it is highly profitable. One other thing, though: it doesn't show commercials. That's right. One of the foundations of TCM is that movies are uncut and commercial free. You turn on TCM, and you will not see one ad for one non-TCM product.[6] Sure, Turner takes a revenue hit on this. Instead of two revenue streams—ad revenue and cable operator fees—the brand just has one, the fees. Yet it is still a money-maker, and it's available on virtually every cable and satellite system in the nation.

But the decision to be commercial free is intentional: it's about being true to the brand and its relationship with its viewers. Again, it starts with the product experience. Gregor adds, "What truly makes us different, better, and more special than any other network is what I like to call context and curation."

Gregor describes "context and curation" as going beyond the movies that TCM chooses to show. At TCM, curation is defined as scheduling movies together in such a way that the viewer might "learn something, feel something, and understand the context as to why the movie is on TCM." Gregor adds, "Every day is a film festival at TCM." Every day is built around a specific subject, whether it is an actor or actress, a director, a genre or setting, a time frame (for example, long weekends), or a theme (such as the Need for Speed). The key is that TCM puts these movies together in an authentic way. The viewer's job is often to determine why some movies are included and some are excluded. Gregor says, "For our fan base, it makes for a fascinating place for ongoing discussions about what we left in and what we left out. They will communicate back to us that we should have included this movie or not included that movie, for a myriad of reasons. But that is what makes them intrigued and coming back for more. We become a place that encourages discussion about classic movies."

TCM is all about authenticity. Movies are not manipulated in any way—no shortening of the credits, no colorizing black-and-white films, no cuts or censoring. This means that unlike movies on other nonsubscription cable channels, you're going to get uncensored nudity, violence, and profanity. The movies are also presented in their original screen aspect ratio. TCM follows through on this authenticity in the movies it chooses to show within a theme. You aren't just going to get the great movies. Gregor says, "How is a classic defined? If we're having a daylong festival on Katherine Hepburn, we don't just play her great movies. She made some stinkers too! If we don't show her less popular movies, then we aren't being an authentic leader in the curated space. It is what generates the dialogue between us and our fans." If TCM were to play just "the hits," it would be essentially cheating on the TCM viewer—going against the brand promise. So it doesn't.

But the brand experience doesn't stop there, because the goal of TCM is to provide insight into each film that viewers might not have had. The goal is to enable the viewer to discover something new about the films—inside scoops, challenges in making the film that were unknown to viewers at the time the film was released, the influence that this particular film had on current movies. (For example, did you know that the Star Wars light-saber scenes are taken directly from the original 1938 Robin Hood film starring Errol Flynn?) Before every film that TCM shows, small vignettes featuring longtime host Robert Osborne, who shares stories behind the making and context of the film, offer additional insight for viewers.

The TCM Viewer

If I asked you who the TCM core viewer is, I bet you'd immediately get a vision of a specific person: probably someone who was alive during World War II and who is spending her golden years in front of the TV watching old movies that were popular in her youth. Although that represents one group of TCM fans, they are a relatively small minority.

One of the first things that Jeff Gregor did when he inherited the TCM brand was to engage in consumer research to better understand the estimated sixty-two million viewers who tuned into the station at least once a month. He did a consumer segmentation study augmented by qualitative research in which he grouped the TCM consumer base by what viewers found important within the channel, including their movie-watching needs and their movie-watching habits. What Gregor found was remarkable.

First, TCM fandom wasn't about age. In fact, two-thirds of its viewers were between the ages of eighteen and forty-nine. Demographically they were well educated, split 50-50 by gender, and in the upper-middle income range. But as is so often the case when we're talking about the brand-consumer relationship, the makeup of the consumers who were in love with the brand went way beyond demographics. They shared similar psychographic characteristics as well as attitudinal and cultural similarities that cut across their physical features. If you were to summarize these viewers, they all had one thing in common: they celebrated classic movies.

TCM's core consumers, its influencers, are nicknamed "Cultural Engagers." They are extremely passionate about and involved in classic films. They pay attention to the details, seek out knowledge and do research about classic films, and want to understand why they matter. They connect socially to the brand. They talk with other movie fans about movies, their meaning, their relevance, and their influence on movies today. They are interested in cinematography and how it has progressed over the years. They want to know how more current movies like *Hugo*, *War Horse*, and *The Artist* have been influenced by classic movies. More important, they want to belong to a community in which they can discuss movies with others. They are the ones whom others go to for movie knowledge and little-known facts. These viewers meet the classic characteristics of influencers.

A secondary group is nicknamed "Relevance Seekers." They look for movies to connect with them in a personally relevant way. They appreciate classic movies and their applicability in today's culture. These are the ones who love to quote dialogue and imitate scenes. They look for a pop culture tie-in. They want "content with a coolness factor" that can be associated with life in the twenty-first century. They see the movie experience as connected to their personal lives.

Creating a Community

The foundation of TCM's brand would be to relentlessly focus on creating a community that would revolve around the sharing and celebrating of classic movies with the Cultural Engager and the Relevance Seeker. The brand would reflect the Engagers' belief that classic movies are as relevant today as they were when they were first released. Gregor notes, "Classic movies are timeless. The actors are as popular today as they were back when the movies were made." He's right. At number five, John Wayne ranks higher on the Harris Poll's 2012 list of favorite actors than either George Clooney or Will Smith.[7]

The TCM community would be defined as a fan group that came together to enjoy classic movies and be inspired and enriched by TCM. Perhaps most important, his community would engage in a two-way dialogue with the brand. Gregor adds, "TCM would provide context and curation, and the

Cultural Engagers would not just be the brand's advocates, but also the jury on how the brand performed. If we did something wrong or weren't authentic in their mind, they'd let us know. It was one group feeding off the other."

To appeal to this core group, TCM has created a channel with the most diverse and largest film portfolio anywhere, representing every major studio. Gregor says that the Cultural Engager views these films as works of art and is anxious to learn the secrets behind their creation. He explains, "The people that worked on or were in these films aren't going to be around forever. We wanted to hear their story. Like Steven Spielberg interviewing the survivors of the Holocaust, their story needs to be told before it is too late."

The marriage between TCM and its viewers continues to evolve. In the purest sense of the word, TCM has become a lifestyle brand. The brand goes well beyond the confines of the linear network. It provides a plethora of social benefits to its consumer base. Gregor and his team have expanded the footprint to include an annual classic film festival that TCM holds in the heart of classic Hollywood over a period of four days, with more than one hundred screenings and events shown in multiple venues. Actors, directors, and other key personnel are on hand to provide additional insight and background stories behind the development of the movies. But at the heart of the experience is the community idea, the ability of movie fans and TCM to interact in the Hollywood environment and do what they like to do—talk with like-minded fans about classic movies.

"We hoped the film festival would be a great environment for our fans, and it has been better than we could have ever expected," Gregor explains. The first festival was entirely sold out. There were more than 25,000 attendees during the four-day event. The most expensive tickets were in the highest demand. "It was then that I knew this brand was bigger than any of us thought." The film festival includes a "Road to Hollywood" event with screenings of classic films in major cities during the months leading into the film festival. Other brand extensions include the TCM Classic Cruise and the TCM Classic Film Tour as well as DVDs of classic and unreleased films by noted actors and directors. All of these add up to a brand about which viewers feel passionately. Robert Osborne is considered a legendary host (by TCM fans), and newer host Ben Mankiewicz brings his own unique style to the network. TCM has become so well loved and so passionately followed that some of its biggest fans have tattooed the brand's logo on various parts of their bodies.

Indexing Passion

Jeff Gregor knew that there was a deep passion for his brand among his viewers, but he didn't know how deep. So he commissioned what he describes as a "Passion Index" independent study. Two research suppliers, the THREE Group and Knowledge Networks, specialists in network research, worked with TCM to develop the study. Gregor's hypothesis was that fans of TCM were just as passionate as fans of other top brands. The Passion Index study gives us a good way to measure how strong a brand's romance is with consumers.

The study asked consumers a number of key questions around their passion for brands. These were narrowed down to ten statements that represented the core principles of

Table 6.1 Passion Dimensions and Statements

Dimension	Passion Index Statements
Consumption	I'm always looking for new ways to make this brand a part of my life.
	I can't get enough of this brand.
Connection and Enjoyment	I feel like this brand was created with me in mind.
	This brand inspires me.
	This brand makes my life better/enriches my life.
Community	This brand shares my values and sensibility.
	I feel good when I use this brand.
	I'm loyal to this brand through good times and bad.
Social and Viral Engagement	I enjoy introducing other people to this brand.
	I feel a strong connection with other people who love this brand.

Source: TCM Passion Index study, conducted June 2012.

passion. A Passion Index was created that averaged the scores of each brand across these ten statements and compared them to other brands in the study. The statements were broken down across four key dimensions, as shown in Table 6.1.

Think about the four broader categories and the ten statements that created the overall Passion Index in this study. I would argue that all these statements could be applied to measure one's passion for another individual—just replace the word "brand" with the name of a person. Go through each of the ten statements and think about your own relationship with a special person in your life. It works, right? Look at the dimensions individually and compare them with the interactions in your own relationships. Consumption is all about the physical interactions with the brand—the functional benefits, similar to our physical interactions with others. Connection and enjoyment go a bit deeper. These are the emotional connection points that a consumer derives from the brand, with the key, "I feel like this brand was created with me in mind," as a driving factor. Community is about a deeper sense of commitment to the brand. Personalities and values align. There is a sharing of interests. Finally, social and viral engagement involves the sharing of the brand with others—the ability of the relationship to be part of a larger social context. Think of the WOMM efforts we explored in Chapter Five.

These ten statements provide us a road map for understanding how much passion there is between a consumer and a brand—a way to quantify the strength of a brand's romance with its most passionate consumers. Remember, this is not about absolute size but about the relative strength of a brand's relationship with its biggest fans. Of course, you may define your brand's relationship with the consumer differently and use other statements to represent your own consumer passion index, but in any case, it is important to create a relationship measurement system. How do you use it? For starters, I see three immediate ways:

- *Discover your brand's relationship strengths and weaknesses.* Brands will have both strengths and opportunity areas in their consumer relationships. In TCM's case, when Jeff

Gregor compared all twenty-two brands across the ten statements and four dimensions, he naturally found that some brands had higher rankings than others on various measures. Your brand's score can give you insight into where your brand should possibly focus its marketing efforts. Maybe your brand is strong in consumption relative to other brands, but weaker in social and viral engagement. If it is important for your brand's consumers to have a strong social connection to the brand, then clearly you now know that you need to create instances where consumers want to introduce or share the brand with others in a social setting.

- *Understand how your brand relationship is progressing over time.* As we will discuss later, brand-consumer relationships wax and wane over time. Implementing an ongoing, trended Passion Index–type study can help you identify when and where the relationship might be going off track—well before traditional market or consumer measures may indicate as much. Think of it as preventive relationship medicine; warning signs of more serious issues may pop up with this routine test.

- *Comparison to others.* How does the strength of your brand's relationship with its strongest consumers compare to that of your competitor's? Where do they have an edge over you, and is it something to be worried about? Jeff Gregor compared TCM's Passion Index rating to the brands that he hypothesized had the strongest brand-consumer relationship. He included competitors, but also included brands that he felt had the most passionate relationships. Depending on your relationship objectives, you will most likely have a different list of comparative brands. Nevertheless, it is critical to have ongoing benchmarks in the form of other brands; these will (1) clarify whether those brands are doing something that is significantly increasing or decreasing their Passion Index rating or (2) reveal whether your brand may be facing potential problems bubbling under the surface.

Let's briefly look at the TCM Passion Index results. Recall from earlier in the chapter that it was the second-highest brand on the dimension "I feel like this brand was created with me in mind." When brands were grouped together for the overall Passion Index (average of all four dimensions compared to each other), TCM also fared extremely well. Brands were sorted into four statistically significant separate groups. The top group comprised only one brand, Apple. No surprise. TCM resided in the next group, just under Apple. Brands in this group included the Boston Red Sox, *Mad Men*, Disney, the NFL, Amazon, NASCAR, *The Simpsons*, and Target.

What do these brands have in common? Some would be considered big (Disney, the NFL, Amazon, and Target); others (the Red Sox, TCM, and *Mad Men*) would be considered smaller but more passionately followed. One thing is clear: despite their relative size, they focus almost all of their marketing efforts on their core consumer.

Specifically, they focus on that consumer's experience. We continually see that brands which have a strong, positive, memorable experiential element associated with them will be the ones most loved and cherished. They make their consumers feel special and take care to engage in real and meaningful interactions with them. It's the surest path to achieving a solid romance.

TCM, like other strong brands, does not rest on its laurels. It is continually refreshing and evolving its product to keep its relationship strong with consumers. The brand has adopted such innovations as the "TCM Guest Programmer," in which Osborne is joined by celebrity guest programmers, such as Spike Lee, Ellen Barkin, and Regis Philbin. Extending from the success of the *Essentials* showcase, which spotlights a different movie and contains a special pre- and postmovie discussion, TCM has created programming to appeal to the next generation of classic movie viewers. It is called *Essentials Jr.*, which adopts the same format but is focused on children and family films. Finally, TCM develops original content, which consists of both documentaries about notable films and classic movie personalities as well as a series filmed in front of a studio audience that explores artistic film collaborations. Gregor adds, "TCM is a microphone for those Hollywood insiders who want to share their story and their role in classic movies."

• • •

The key lesson in this chapter is that brands must always be evolving their experience, doing so with an eye to the needs and wants of their core consumer base. Innovation is the lifeblood of any brand-consumer relationship. It is the primary way that people's relationships with brands continue to grow. Just as in our own human relationships, if there is a rut and there is little new or different, the relationship will stop growing and eventually suffer. It is critical to offer the consumer new ideas, new messages, and new vistas on what the brand can be. In the next chapter, we will see how brands that have very stable relationships with consumers continue to keep the relationship fresh and exciting through news and innovation.

7

KEEP LOVE ALIVE

The main cafeteria on the campus of St. John's University is quiet on this typically cold New York day, except for the delivery man slowly filling the vending machine. It is getting close to when midday classes will be dismissed, and within minutes the quietness will be erased by the bustling energy of students transitioning from the classroom into the lunchroom. Sure enough, as 11:30 passes by, the dining hall begins filling up with undergraduate students.

That same vending machine, now completely filled, remains quiet on the wall until a young woman comes over to get her lunchtime beverage of choice. She puts her money in, presses the button, and out pops a bottle of Coca-Cola. As she reaches for it, another one pops out. Smiling at her good fortune, she goes to grab that one as well. As she reaches for it, yet another bottle comes out. Looking a bit sheepish now, as this is starting to garner the attention of other cafeteria-goers, she reaches for that one too. Bottles keep coming, faster now. With every drop of a bottle, there is an audible gasp and occasional squeal among the students at nearby tables. She has six in her hand now. She starts giving them away to fellow students, yet the vending machine keeps pushing out bottles of Coke. After she's passed out quite a few, it finally stops.

Another young woman approaches the vending machine, puts in her dollar, pushes the button for a Coke, and receives her Coke bottle. Halfway expecting the machine to repeat its previous performance, she waits for a split second to see if more bottles of Coke will start coming out. As she starts to turn away, out shoots a human hand from the machine's opening, giving her a bouquet of flowers.

A guy wants in on this action. After he puts his dollar in, the machine goes dark and then lights up brightly, Vegas style, with the bells and sirens and beeps that indicate he's won a jackpot. Bottles of Coke fall from the machine like quarters from a winning slot machine. He also starts passing them out to other students. The cafeteria is going crazy now. Students are high-fiving each other and sharing bottles of Coke, with some even giving the vending machine a hug.

Even crazier things start to happen. A bottle of Coke comes out with funky red LED sunglasses attached to it. Two hands appear and start making balloon animals and handing them out (with a Coke of course). A woman goes up to get her Coke, and a large pizza emerges from the vending machine followed by (what else?) a two-liter bottle of Coke. Pizza for everyone! Finally, the machine starts blinking and beeping again, and out comes a six-foot-long submarine sandwich. Students are on their feet, laughing, cheering, and wildly screaming with delight. The small dining hall on St. John's campus has been transformed into a stronghold of happiness. Those students will remember that day forever.

The Coca-Cola Happiness Machine had made its debut. This entire event was documented on hidden camera to share the reactions of these real students (not actors) and the happiness that Coke could bring everywhere. The theme to the execution would be "Where Would Happiness Strike Next?" and it would become a word-of-mouth sensation.

STORYTELLING

How do you keep a 120-something-year-old relationship fresh? That is the challenge that confronts the marketing folks who work on what consistently is the number-one-ranked brand in Interbrand's annual *Best Global Brands Report*. How does a brand like Coca-Cola continue to evolve a relationship? How does the company add to a consumer romance with a brand that was invented the same year that President Cleveland married Francis Folsom in the White House? After all, as Jackie Jantos, former Coca-Cola Company creative director for global content, says, "The product itself—the actual liquid—hasn't innovated in almost 130 years. But that doesn't mean that the relationship can't evolve or innovate."[1]

The Coca-Cola Company isn't shying away from its desire to grow its relationship with the next generation of consumers. It is embracing marketing in the twenty-first century with a strategy that is robustly aggressive yet grounded specifically in enhancing conversations and stories about the brand. This strategy isn't tucked away in some tightly held vault. No, Coke is telling the world exactly how it plans to strengthen an already extremely strong romance with the consumer. In a seventeen-minute video posted online by Jonathan Mildenhall, vice president of global advertising strategy and creative excellence at The Coca-Cola Company, he discusses how Coke will take a core idea that goes back to its origins—storytelling— and enhance it.

As Mildenhall describes it in the video, "Storytelling is at the heart of all families, communities, and cultures."[2] Think about this for a minute. Our lives are a series of stories. Some are good and some are bad. Some have happy endings, and others have sad or tragic ones. Every time you communicate with another individual, you are usually telling a story. There are the mundane stories of how your day went and the exciting stories about a dream that has finally come true. Stories are an integral part of our lives and our relationships. They are an integral part of us. They have also been in the DNA of the Coca-Cola brand since its inception.

Let's go back for a moment to the brand's origins. Coca-Cola was invented by Confederate Colonel John Pemberton in 1886. As Frederick Allen writes in his book *Secret Formula*,

The postwar sharecropper South was a region desperate for remedies of every sort. Most people suffered from inadequate diets, and the poor still subsisted on a so-called white diet of the three M's—meat, meal, and molasses—that led to widespread malnutrition. In rural areas, undrained swamps were like giant petri dishes, crawling with disease. The long, hot Southern summers bred insects, spoiled food, and drove children outside barefoot where they caught hookworm. Many households lacked even the rudimentary sanitation of the outhouse. Confederate veterans returned home with aching, lingering wounds and maladies. On top of it all, the region's poverty and rural isolation led to a grinding, dispiriting boredom that made many Southerners susceptible to the relief found in little brown bottles that contained alcohol or laudanum and other opiates.[3]

Doesn't that sound fun? Well, Pemberton realized that people in the region needed and wanted something that could do a small part in helping them escape the abysmal existence that they were living. They needed, as Coke would put it many years later, a simple moment of pleasure.

Jantos adds, "Think about the story of how Coca-Cola was even invented. Doc Pemberton created it as an uplifting beverage. It continues to do that today. Our job is to encourage stories around liquid happiness because Coke is, in effect, happiness in a bottle." The mission of the Coca-Cola brand has not changed. It has merely evolved. Throughout the history of the brand, happiness has played an integral role. From 1923's "Enjoy Life" to the "Have a Coke and a Smile" campaign in 1979, Coke has been and always will be about happiness. And the job of the marketing team is to take the idea of happiness and encourage stories around liquid happiness in a twenty-first-century kind of way.

Mildenhall's video is called *Coca-Cola Content 2020*, and it lays out how the biggest marketer in the world is going to adapt its relationships with consumers in the twenty-first century. He describes the challenge of content creation in an enlightening way, reminding us that "every contact point with a customer should tell an emotional story." The strategy is called "Liquid and Linked," and it defines Coke's future interaction with consumers. "Liquid" describes ideas so contagious that they cannot be controlled. "Linked" indicates that these stories will create links among the company's business, brands, and consumers. Mildenhall continues, "Through the stories that Coca-Cola tells, we will provoke conversations and a disproportionate share of popular culture."[4]

What Mildenhall is describing isn't just stories for stories' sake. Coke will employ what it calls *dynamic storytelling*, which in essence involves Coke engaging in storytelling with consumers in a way that not only intrigues them but also gives them something to talk about with friends and family. Coke will begin the stories, but the ultimate goal is for the consumer to take those stories and run with them. After all, the company has done research and knows that 80 percent of the Coca-Cola brand stories out there didn't come from Coke's messaging. Coke is going to embrace that fact and build on it. It will encourage more sharing and more telling of stores. Nowhere was this better evidenced than in the "Where Will Happiness Strike Next?" online vignettes (like the one at St. John's University) starring the Happiness Machine.

Defining Happiness

"Where Will Happiness Strike Next?" was the first online execution of Coke's new "Open Happiness" brand campaign, which had been introduced in 2009. The new positioning essentially put a new context around what Coke had been doing for years—starting with a simple moment of pleasure. Remember that one thing that a brand should own?

Coca-Cola's is happiness. The beauty of Coke's brand essence is that it aligns so well with the physical product and the emotional uplift that the brand provides.

But what exactly is happiness, and how can it be communicated? In short, the idea of happiness cuts across all people in all societies. There is physical happiness, emotional happiness, and cultural happiness. In fact, Coke went so far as to come up with five drivers of happiness that would be a part of any brand communication:

- Be active
- Be together
- Discover
- Be in the now
- Be giving

Remember when we said early on that a relationship is defined by two parties giving to each other? Well, Coke wanted to stop talking about happiness. Instead, Coke wanted to *share* a happiness experience with others and celebrate that happiness. If Coke could provide happiness experiences, consumers would tell more stories, and those stories would ultimately spread across the landscape.

Of course, being Coca-Cola, the new "Open Happiness" campaign would be executed in a big way, with emphasis on Super Bowl ads and heavy promotion. This time, however, there would also be a digital component, though compared to everything else that would be supporting the happiness initiative, it would be decidedly small. A. J. Brustein, Coca-Cola senior brand manager, explains it this way: "Our strategy was to leverage the power of our fans to spread our content and our message. The experiment was to see if we could do that without putting any money behind trying to make it viral."[5] In the *Coca-Cola Content 2020* video, Mildenhall explains that Coca-Cola had a distinctive marketing spending model that allocated marketing funds basically as follows:

- 70 percent of investment would be in proven activation tools (advertisements, new packaging, promotions, and so on)
- 20 percent of investment would be on innovations to proven activation tools (new ways to share an advertisement, new types of point-of-sale on shelf, and the like)
- 10 percent would be on completely new, experimental tools

The "Where Will Happiness Strike Next?" initiative was clearly seen as experimental. Brustein recalls, "It was something that definitely would have fit in the 10 percent. Only about five or six people in the company even knew about it!"

Spreading Happiness

When it came time to create a plan to engage with consumers online, Brustein called on a promotion veteran who had gone back and forth between The Coca-Cola Company and assorted agencies for the previous twenty years. Christy Amador had always been a bit of a rogue at the traditional Coca-Cola Company. She had been known to push the envelope, but had also led some of the more innovative Coca-Cola programs in recent history. She would be the perfect person to take on a nontraditional campaign.

The first thing that Amador quickly understood was that if you wanted to create something organic that consumers would genuinely want to pass along, you couldn't do what Coke historically liked to do in its messaging—control it. Amador says, "We wanted to create an experience that would surprise and delight people with authentic happiness. We weren't going to control it. If we looked like we were controlling it, then we would lose all credibility."[6] It was a slippery slope. All too often, marketers put out what they hope will drive consumer pass-along. Most of the time, however, these messages are just too commercial to create any desire for the consumer to forward them on to others. Of course, there were exceptions to this. The Toyota Sienna, with its "Swagger Wagon" online music videos, and Skittles, with its "Touch the Rainbow" executions, followed the unwritten rule that if you wanted to interact virally, you needed to hand your messaging over to consumers and let them run with it. If Coke was to succeed, the content would need to be humorous and engaging if they wanted a viewer to pass it on.

This brings us to that winter day in 2011 when the Happiness Machine first appeared on the St. John's campus and the experience with unknowing students was captured by hidden camera. Because the camera was hidden, everything about the experience was accurately portrayed, including the students' genuine reactions. The romance between consumer and brand was on full display. Jantos describes it as being "simple, intimate Coke moments." Amador adds, "It had to be authentic. It had to be real. We had to capture people's real emotions in real time."

And what was even more unusual about the experience? Jantos explains, "We saw people's true goodness. They shared things. If five bottles of Coke came out of the vending machine, they shared them with their friends. We were capturing the idea that sharing brings happiness not just to others but to you too."

The ending message of "Where Will Happiness Strike Next?" created a buzz factor in the form of anticipation that the Happiness Machine might come to your town. In fact, the campaign's popularity prompted Coke to respond with a touring Happiness Machine sampling program that mimicked the experience that had gone viral.

The other unique thing about the campaign was that it was very un-Cokelike in that it didn't have a large national media budget. It grew organically. Coke launched it on social media sites and its own website, but a majority of "spreading" was done by consumers themselves. To say that the message took on a life of its own would be an understatement. According to Amador, to date, the original "Where Will Happiness Strike Next?" vignette has been has been viewed online by a total of twenty-five million people worldwide, reminding every viewer why he or she has a relationship with Coca-Cola. The campaign proved to be so popular online that Coke cut television commercials from the footage and aired them on such popular shows as the *American Idol* finale. Amador estimates that over one hundred million people have seen a version of the "Where Will Happiness Strike Next?" TV commercial. In that same time, Coke's Facebook fans have increased from 3.7 million to more than 60 million. The online film itself won a slew of awards, including the Gold Clio Award, National Addy Award, and Gold

Telly; was a finalist at the Cannes International Film Festival; and won *Advertising Age*'s Small Agency Campaign of the Year. In addition, the campaign hit *Visual Measurers* Top 10 for views and was named the Top Viral Video by *Creativity Online*.

INNOVATION ENHANCES ROMANCE

Why did the "Where Will Happiness Strike Next?" campaign work? A few reasons:

- *It was unexpected.* Amador states, "Whenever Coke does something, it usually does it in a huge way. Big sampling programs, huge TV campaigns, large scale promotions. This was different. This was so personal, so intimate. It showcased the brand and the consumer interacting on a one-on-one basis. For Coke to show up at a small university cafeteria on a random day was so different from what you would normally expect from Coke."

- *It stayed true to its origins.* Brustein explains, "Because so few people knew about it, we didn't have to pass this by a committee and make it 'safe.' It stayed true to what it was. It stayed true to the idea." This is important. Coke innovated through a unique web experience. Yet this experience stayed on strategy; it stayed true to the message. All too often we use innovation in a nonstrategic way, designed to wow and dazzle at the expense of staying on brand message. Don't let this happen! Find innovations that are aligned with the core essence yet add excitement to the relationship. If something isn't on strategy, don't move forward with it.

- *It was authentic.* Jantos notes, "There was an innocence [about the scene]. There was simplicity of the past. In the setting, you don't see a lot of technologically intense stuff. It's a mealtime. It's a cafeteria. It's not modern at all, so in a way, it took the brand back to its roots." Again, the message stays true to the authenticity of Coca-Cola.

- *It used social media and online activation in the right way.* Many marketers view social media as the new Holy Grail to connecting with the consumer and are all too often disappointed with the results. Coke didn't rely on social media alone to carry the message. It used online videos to build on an already established message and to carry that message out in a way that fit well with the online space. The story was entertaining. It was fun. But it also didn't try to shove Coke down your throat. Yes, Coke was a part of it, but the stars of the vignettes were consumers themselves and their genuine reactions to what was coming out of that vending machine. It wasn't some contrived marketing execution.

- *Most important, it connected emotionally.* Amador says, "It was so important to capture the emotions and reactions of people. We were able to do that, and it became a message that others wanted to share." "Where Will Happiness Strike Next?" was a tangible human expression of happiness that was executed in a medium that allowed for it to be *shared*. At its core, that's what Coke is about: sharing that simple moment of pleasure with others. Go back to the classic Coke commercials. From Mean Joe Green to the young people on the hillside singing that they'd like to buy the world a Coke, Coke always has been about the sharing of happiness. People desire happiness, and they desire to pass it along to others. This was why the Happiness Machine message was compelling enough to spread. It also shows that no brand is too old or too outdated to engage in furthering the romance with its user base.

• • •

Unexpectedness, innovation, news—these are all ways that both new and mature brands can grow with consumers. That 10 percent of the marketing budget that Coke spends on radically new innovations is disproportionately critical to the future of its business. In fact, Coke readily admits this by indicating that although the innovation budget is only 10 percent of the whole, the amount of thinking required to fuel those initiatives is substantially higher.[7] These initiatives serve as the platforms on which future innovations will build. They're part of a never-ending cycle.

Innovation can take many forms and play many roles. Here are just a few examples:

- *News ways to communicate.* This would include leveraging technology in both creative execution and message delivery.
- *New packaging, logos, and looks.* We all desire makeovers from time to time; brands are no exception.
- *Extensions and flankers.* New twists and changes to our existing products can help further communicate what our brand is all about.
- *New locations and places to interact.* This includes the discovery of new places for consumers to find our brands and

partnerships with new channels and outlets to sell our products.

- *New associations or new representatives.* New sponsorship properties or events or even celebrities enable the brand to change its proposition or personality.
- *New products.* Beyond just line extensions, innovations often come in the form of new products that become part of the brand. This is especially true in any category that is subject to frequent technological or design advances. Brands sometimes find that changes or improvements are needed to continue to grow the relationship with the consumer. How often does Nike change the design of its shoes? Almost annually. There's nothing wrong with the current model, but to be on the cutting edge both in performance and fashion, Nike will continue to create.

INNOVATION TO ESCAPE RELATIONSHIP "RUTS"

In 2010, Domino's Pizza, a brand whose consumer relationship was in a rut, did something unthinkable. In fact, it executed two radical strategies simultaneously. First, the company changed its pizza recipe. For a mainstream branded pizza product, this was a big deal.

It didn't stop there. Along with the new pizza recipe, Domino's launched a campaign that featured consumers talking about how awful the pizza was that the company had been serving them for the past fifty years. In the ads, Domino's shared hidden-camera consumer feedback to introduce the new pizza. For years, brands have introduced "new and improved" products, but no brand has ever been this forthright in admitting that the product it had previously marketed was inferior. There was significant risk to this approach. Would consumers be upset, considering that Domino's was admitting that it had essentially been intentionally serving terrible pizza and taking their money? But the results were quite different. In launching the campaign, Domino's became more transparent than any brand ever had. The Domino's website picked up everything that consumers were saying about the brand in the social media space—good, bad, and indifferent—and broadcast it right on its website. The results were unreal: both Domino's profit and its stock price rose over 200 percent in the year following the campaign launch.[8] An old, somewhat outdated brand was able to escape a relationship rut through an improvement of its pizza recipe. But the innovative way that this change was communicated, openly and honestly, resulted in a complete renewal of its romance with the consumer.

Product innovations can breathe new life into a brand-consumer relationship. Innovation may require marketers to take risks both professionally and personally. In 1985, Procter & Gamble's (P&G) Bounty paper towels were in trouble. Paper towels had basically been commoditized. They all looked the same; they were either white or solid dye colors. And although Bounty had long lived on the functional strength of being the "quicker picker upper," the brand had not done enough to create a romance with the consumer for it to command any more value (in terms of pricing) than any other paper towel brand. This was happening to P&G across a number of categories, and upper management issued a charge to all employees: pursue breakthrough product innovation.

Emmett Leopardi was, at that time, an engineer in the P&G paper division. One day, he was walking the paper towel aisle at the supermarket and almost picked up a competitive product because there were no differences among any of the brands. An idea struck him. Bounty had to make a radical change if it was going to continue to have a loyal consumer base. He says, "We needed to do something that for the paper towel category would be akin to what the color TV did for the television industry."[9]

Leopardi's thought was that the moms who used these towels day in and day out needed something to brighten their day. "Moms would be doing these mundane tasks with paper towels, cleaning, putting them in lunches, whatever. I just wanted to give them a small gift to brighten their day when they used the towels." That gift would be in the form of printed decorative designs on the paper towels. P&G middle management did not support the idea. Even the marketing team was dubious. Leopardi was told that he was an engineer and didn't understand the consumer mind-set, which they believed was concerned only about functional benefits, such as absorbency and strength.

Still, Leopardi, moonlighting and without management support, pursued color photography printed on Bounty paper. When he discovered that the process worked, he knew he had to share what he had been doing with P&G senior management, but also let them know that he had been doing this without company approval. P&G management agreed that the idea had merit and put him in charge of the project. According to the Leopardi Group website, Leopardi and his team created a printed Bounty concept that received some of the highest scores ever in company history. Bounty paper towels had created a newsworthy innovation. Today, printed-design paper towels represent over half of all paper towels sold in the category.

Innovation almost always requires taking risks. Risks are never comfortable, and, by definition, never guaranteed success. In fact, many innovations fail. If we never take risks, our relationships with consumers will ultimately suffer. There is a difference between developing innovations just to be different and taking a "smart risk"—a thought-out, calculated risk, which will involve doing what this book has been preaching: understanding consumers—their functional and emotional needs, their desires, and their goals—and ensuring that the innovation will meet those needs in a way that is different than existing products.

Of course innovation can also play a role in rescuing a relationship that has been ignored. It can breathe new life into brands that were out of consumers' thoughts for years, as we'll see in the next section.

Reconnecting

As Blake Hawley was crossing the street, she noticed the blue flashing lights of a slowly moving squad car coming toward her. After that came cars with their lights on, again moving as though in a slow-motion film sequence. As the cars continued to pass by, she saw it: the long, black limousine following behind. She did a double take. Was there someone famous in town? The president? The governor? But this wasn't a limo. Rather, the car in question was a hearse en route to the local cemetery in a funeral procession. Blake sighed to herself, *Another Geritol customer lost.*

Hawley was the director of marketing for a specialty pharmaceutical company, Meda Consumer Healthcare (MCH), which was part of the larger international Meda AB, an international pharmaceutical company. Her job was to reengage consumers with long-forgotten brands that MCH had acquired. Geritol was the centerpiece of this strategy. It would also be the most challenging. Blake and the brand manager on Geritol, Cigdem Topalli, would have to bring back to life a brand that hadn't been marketed heavily since the 1970s.

Jeffrey Cohen, VP and general manager of MCH, is an optimist. He has to be. His job is to find brands that have been left for dead, acquire them for a small fraction of what they were once worth, and rebuild their value. Cohen's team is tasked with purchasing brands that were at one time top brands in their respective categories. As he puts it, "These brands are either at death's door or on life support just waiting for the plug to be pulled. Our job is to resurrect these brands—by investing in what was once a strong relationship with the consumer."[10] His stable of brands looks like a pharmaceutical hall of fame and includes Feosol, an iron supplement first launched in 1941; Geritol (launched in 1952); and relative newbies Contact Cold & Flu (1961) and Vivarin Caffeine Alertness Aid (1968).

All these brands have been on steady declines for many years, their relationships with consumers badly managed, ignored, or neglected. Nevertheless, when searching for these brands and in choosing the brands that were purchased, Cohen indicates that there is often a ray of sunshine amid the gloomy brand numbers. It becomes a fascinating process.

For MCH to consider purchasing a brand that most would never touch, the brand has to meet a few key criteria. It goes without stating that the business fundamentals—cash flow, spend, profitability—have to be worthwhile. If the brand has been so mismanaged that it is losing money, MCH won't pursue it. Only those brands that have positive cash flow and profitability can make the initial cut.

But for Cohen and his team to get really excited about a potential brand, it has to show that it has some goodwill among a fickle consumer base. Usually these are brands that were once marketed very heavily but then have been undermarketed or ignored completely in recent years. People have some awareness, and there is some measure of good feeling toward the brand, even if they can't specifically identify it as a good feeling. Cohen notes, "If people have awareness and a reservoir of goodwill, we can reinvent the relationships with these consumers." He adds, "Many of these brands were even beyond being milked for cash. The companies who owned them were essentially saying, 'We don't care about these brands.'"

The final checkpoint for the MCH team is that the product itself is at least at parity in formulation with other competitors. MCH's brands fit this criterion, in part due to FTC compliance requirements in the over-the-counter (OTC) pharmaceutical industry. Cohen says, "Contact has all the cold ingredients that you would expect in a cold medicine. Feosol is a parity iron supplement, and Vivarin has 200 mg of caffeine per tablet, which is standard in the industry. The only product that is remarkably different than some of its competitors is Geritol. We had to address that."

In short, the brands that MCH purchases are the equivalent of dogs available for adoption at a local pound. There is a lot of history there, and maybe some of it isn't great. Although the brands have all seen better days, there is still enough of a spark, enough potential, to convince the team that with a little love and care, these brands can, in fact, still thrive and actively engage in relationships with key consumer groups.

Cohen indicates that when MCH purchases a brand, its immediate task is to stop the decline. "We know that there are good feelings from consumers about these brands, and we need to understand where those feelings emanate. That takes a bit of time to figure out. But we also know that we have an ongoing business to run that we can't just ignore while we reposition and re-launch these brands. We employ a short- and long-term strategy." Essentially the short-term strategy is to do whatever it takes to keep the brands on the store shelves until a more robust positioning effort can be crafted and executed. MCH makes retailers a promise: Cohen will tell them, "We know this brand is struggling. We are going to figure out how to reinvent it and create a relationship with the consumer that is relevant." In the meantime, MCH requests that the retailer keep it on the shelf and drive volume with short-term promotions until the new plan can be figured it out. No other brand has had more of a challenge in reinventing itself than Geritol.

Modernizing an Oldie

Given that she had all of MCH's wayward brands under her belt, Blake Hawley knew that Geritol would require someone special. She knew exactly whom to put on it. When Cigdem Topalli was given the Geritol brand management assignment, she was excited. She had been working her entire career to get into the brand management arena and had recently transferred from MCH's pharmaceutical marketing group into the OTC/ consumer brand management team. So when the assignment came through, she was naturally ready to tell everyone. She explains, "I realized that this brand might have a problem when I asked my sixty-seven-year-old mother-in-law if she wanted any samples, and she told me that she didn't take Geritol because that was for old people."[11]

The Meda team soon realized that Geritol was trapped in a time warp in which neither the product nor the marketing had changed in fifty years. In its consumer relationships, it had issues aplenty. Its image was outdated, and there was concern as to whether the product was even relevant in the second decade of the second millennium.

Let's start with the imagery. Geritol wasn't just perceived as old. It was seen as ancient. It was completely outdated. Take the name. The "Geri" prefix immediately connoted that this was a brand for geriatric women. We're not talking recently retired women. Consumers saw Geritol as a brand that would be available in assisted living homes. The advertising, or lack thereof, hadn't helped either. Geritol had talked to its consumers quite frequently in the 1950s, communicating to housewives with a campaign that promoted Geritol as a remedy for tiredness and "iron-poor blood" and featuring such young and upcoming stars as Betty White. In the 1950s, the brand was everywhere. It was heavily advertised, and it sponsored variety shows. The problem was that the brand had stayed in the 1950s. Beyond a brief attempt in the 1970s to age down the brand with thirty-something spokespeople such as baseball player Steve Garvey, his wife, Cyndi, and tennis player Evonne Goolagong, the brand essentially went dark and stopped communicating with the consumer altogether. In short, the brand had literally been lost in time.

Topalli says, "It had become a joke. Geritol was given out at retirement parties and was a signal that you were old." Hawley adds, "Even our current users, who raved about the product, didn't want anyone to know that they were taking it. One woman told us that she had to hide it from her husband because she didn't want him to think that she was getting older."[12] The brand's meaning was so lost from years of neglect that in the early 2000s, an urban myth arose that Geritol was a secret fertility drug.

Hawley and Topalli had a huge task on their hands. MCH had bought Geritol because the financials were strong and there was enough brand awareness built in that could still be accessed. However, it was essential to put into place a marketing plan to modernize the brand to begin a relationship with a younger consumer.

The team started with the product itself. Geritol came in two forms, Geritol Complete, a multivitamin, and Geritol Tonic, a liquid version that featured iron and B vitamins. Topalli looked first at the multivitamin Geritol Complete product because it was clearly the bigger opportunity. The OTC vitamin category was a $3.5 billion category, driven by multivitamins. So she compared Geritol's ingredient label with that of a leading brand. What they saw is shown in Table 7.1.

Do you notice anything that would concern you if you were the brand manager of Geritol? Of course you do: with the exception of Vitamin A, for every vitamin, Centrum exceeds Geritol, often by a significant amount. If you had an ingredient

Table 7.1 Percentage of RDA: Geritol vs. Centrum Silver

Ingredient	Geritol Complete % RDA	Centrum Silver % RDA
Vitamin A	120	70
Vitamin B-6	100	250
Vitamin B-12	110	833
Vitamin C	100	167
Vitamin D	100	200
Vitamin E	100	117
Vitamin K	30	67

panel that looks like this and wanted to be seen as a credible competitor, what would you do?

You would probably immediately want to reformulate the product to get it to parity or even to exceed the category leader. If a competitor has almost eight times the amount of Vitamin B-12 that you have, that puts you at a pretty big disadvantage, right? How could Geritol ever change consumer perception that it was an outdated brand when the product formulation was so inferior to that of the leading brand? Talk about 1950s!

But Geritol wasn't going to reformulate. The team was actually quite happy with the Geritol formulation. Why? Look at the ingredient panel again. If you analyze Geritol, you'll notice that the brand stays very close to the RDA percentage. It is remarkably consistent across all vitamins.

Geritol wasn't going to try to "out-megadose" the competition. Why not? There were two reasons. First, MCH wouldn't be able to out-formulize a category that contained ten mega brands driven by two large companies with deep pockets. Second, and more important, was a reason that directly affected consumers. The vitamin category was operating under a fallacy that implied that the more vitamins a person took, the better off he or she was. That wasn't necessarily the case. In fact, there were reports and features by such prominent advocates as Dr. Oz that consumers were, in fact, megadosing themselves. The Geritol team would stay with their formula and claim that they had a *balanced* formula. This was something different. It was something they could own. Geritol gave you just what you needed to lead a vital life—nothing more, nothing less. In other words, Geritol's balanced formula enabled the consumer to lead a balanced life.

The team quickly tested the "balance" idea with both the existing Geritol consumer base and a younger generation of women (fifty- to fifty-five-year-olds). Surprisingly, across the board, the younger consumers responded more strongly to the "well-balanced" message. It fit with their perception of the Geritol brand and was seen to have the potential to make an impact.

All of a sudden, Geritol could adopt a new core influencer to romance. She would be a healthy, active, vibrant woman in her fifties. Cigdem says, "We were going to change from being perceived as a brand for someone like Betty White to one for someone like Jamie Lee Curtis."

Hawley adds, "The new overarching essence behind the brand would be physical and mental vitality. The reason why we were able to provide this vitality to our consumers would be our well-balanced formula combined with an exciting and vibrant personality. The formula itself represented balance." It was classic laddering—using product attributes to support compelling functional and emotional benefits. Of course, there would be a significant amount of work to do. Geritol had negative social cachet, if any, and little in the way of brand personality.

The plan would be implemented in two stages. Stage one would be to stabilize the base business. Stage two would be to reestablish and, in many cases, create a new relationship with the consumer through brand innovation. Topalli says, "If we did our job right in stage one, we would prove ourselves to both our consumers and retailers. Both would be receptive to future news and innovation around the brand."

To start, they would give the Geritol packaging a new look. It hadn't been changed in at least ten years and reinforced the perception that Geritol was old and outdated. For example, the liquid version of the product was still referred to as a "tonic"—hardly twenty-first-century vernacular. Packaging changes stayed true to the brand's heritage (for example, the color red was kept), but the old-fashioned look was gone, replaced by a more contemporary look that helped communicate the new balanced/vitality positioning. "Tonic" was replaced with "Liquid" and Geritol Complete was renamed Geritol Multivitamin.

The team implemented a comprehensive plan to talk with consumers for the first time in thirty years. It included advertising in magazines like *Good Housekeeping* and *Ladies Home Journal*, and, for the first time in decades, Geritol would be seen on television. Geritol ads would run on national cable outlets like Lifetime, Hallmark, and the Cooking Channel. To develop a brand experience, an association would be implemented around key fitness walks around the country that support important health causes for women. Hawley notes, "Being physically active is a part of life balance. Walking isn't extreme and isn't intense, but it is so essential for good health. It bridges all ages of women."

The brand was successful at stabilizing the business. In year one, even prior to any packaging or messaging changes, Geritol stopped declining and actually grew. But the brand team has larger goals. Topalli articulates the ultimate goal as follows: "We want women to understand that Geritol needs to be an everyday part their lives so that they can continue to maintain that vibrant lifestyle. It is something to take to help you live energetically versus something to take so you won't die. We want our consumers not to see Geritol as an embarrassment, but be proud to have it in their medicine cabinet. My hope is that Geritol emerges as the ultimate comeback brand."

Hawley articulates the goal more succinctly: "We're putting this brand in a place so that when I do see a hearse go by, I don't worry that I've lost yet another consumer."

THE POWER OF INNOVATION

Even if their relationship is in a mature stage with consumers, the strongest brands, like Coca-Cola, continue to innovate and change. They must to survive. Think about human relationships. They are nurtured and can develop when we keep things exciting and new. We have enriching experiences together and grow together; we don't just stay the same people throughout our lives. Nor can a brand stay stagnant with its consumer base. Without ongoing streams of news, the relationship inevitably starts to plateau. If the communication simply stops, the brand ends up in crisis mode, as Geritol did, where something drastic must be done.

Of course the Geritol example is a case of a long period of brand neglect that drove the need for radical innovation. That being said, there are often instances when an immediate, sudden incident will affect the relationship dramatically. Crises emerge in the life of every brand-consumer relationship. Relationships are never smooth. How the brand responds to the crisis and how the crisis is resolved will affect the future of the brand-consumer relationship. We'll examine that next.

8

MAKING UP

For any Atlanta Falcon fan—actually, for any NFL fan—the scene was surreal. On that cold evening of December 11, 2007, the local Atlanta NBC news affiliate WXIA went to a live feed featuring the Falcons' football coach, Bobby Petrino, not in Atlanta but in Fayetteville, Arkansas, home of the University of Arkansas, doing the "Sooey Pig" Razorback cheer. Just twenty-four hours earlier, Petrino had coached the Falcons to their tenth loss of the season, a 34-14 drubbing by the New Orleans Saints. Now, alongside his wife and kids, he was raising his hands and squealing like a pig at an Arkansas Razorback pep rally. Earlier that morning, he'd resigned his Falcons job and, just as quickly, taken a position as coach of the Razorbacks. With three games remaining in a disastrous 2007 season, the Falcons had no head football coach.

They also had lost their brand. Petrino's "sooey" squeal capped what was a bizarre turn of events for an Atlanta Falcons franchise that three years earlier had played in the NFC title game. At the start of 2007, Petrino had signed a five-year, $24 million contract with the Falcons and come on board with lofty expectations. Previously, as the head coach of the University of Louisville, Petrino had compiled a 41-9 record and was considered an offensive genius whose teams were routinely some of the highest scoring in the nation. The Atlanta Falcons brought him on to be paired with their All-Pro, All-Franchise, All-World quarterback, Michael Vick. With blistering speed and a powerful arm, Vick had dramatically changed the way the quarterback position was played in the NFL.

In 2006, the year before Petrino arrived, Vick became the first quarterback in the history of the NFL to rush for over a thousand yards. In Vick, the Falcons had a player most football insiders pegged as the most gifted athlete in the NFL. Now he was going to be teamed up with Petrino, the offensive genius.

The Falcons' team management was anticipating a dream season. According to Jim Smith, Falcons chief marketing officer, "We were on the verge of being one of the most popular franchises in the NFL, and it was all built around Michael Vick."[1] You couldn't pick up a magazine, watch a sporting event, or drive on the highway without seeing Vick's image. He had landed endorsement deals with Nike, EA Sports, Coca-Cola, Powerade, Kraft, Rawlings, Hasbro, and AirTran, to name a few. At the end of 2006, *Sports Illustrated* estimated Vick's income between his NFL salary and his endorsement deals at $25.4 million, ranking him tenth in a listing of highest-earning athletes in the world.[2]

Everything was in place for a run at the Super Bowl and the elimination of the stigma of being one of the NFL's doormats since the franchise's inaugural 3-11 season of 1966. In fact, in their forty-one seasons of playing professional football, the Falcons had never put together two winning seasons in a row. But this was about to change. Petrino plus Vick would surely equal a Super Bowl championship.

Those dreams would quickly vanish. On April 25, 2007, a search warrant was executed that led to evidence of unlawful dogfighting at a property owned by Vick in rural Surry County, Virginia. It was soon discovered that Vick was in charge of an operation that resulted in the gruesome abuse, torture, and execution of dogs that weren't up to "fighting standards." Animal rights activists and public outrage soon followed, and Vick was indicted in July on felony charges of operating an interstate dogfighting venture known as Bad Newz Kennels. Vick entered a guilty plea on August 24, 2007, and, just hours later, was suspended indefinitely, without pay, by the NFL. On December 10, just twenty-four hours before Petrino's shocking departure from the team, Vick was sentenced to twenty-three months in federal prison. Michael Vick, the Falcons' offensive savior and golden ticket to becoming a legitimate football team—a legitimate football *brand*—was effectively done as an Atlanta Falcon.

FINDING THE BRAND

On that cold December evening, in the span of little more than twenty-four hours, the Atlanta Falcons franchise had hit bottom. The Falcons brand was on life support. According to Smith, "Even prior to Michael Vick, our brand had never been that strong. The way we played football was the complete opposite of what our consumer base was interested in. The South loves football, but the South also likes traditional football. You run the ball, you pass the ball, you play good defense. If you had asked someone to define our brand prior to the Michael Vick era, they wouldn't have said traditional southern football. Our brand would be defined as inconsistent football and losing seasons. Even with Michael Vick, we played nontraditional football."

He was right. The Falcons brand and, more important, its relationship with its fan base were built upon the shallow foundation of trick plays, losing seasons, and significant miscalculations in both talent and coaching that had led to an inferior on-the-field experience throughout the team's history. Prior to the Michael Vick era, the Falcons employed Jerry Glanville as their head coach. Glanville was about as nontraditional as they came, dressed all in black and sporting a black cowboy hat, outfitting the team in black uniforms, and running a complicated high-octane "run and shoot" offense that was more sizzle than steak. The team never had a brand persona that attracted as large a fan base as it should have, considering that Atlanta is the ninth-largest city in the United States. The closest the Falcons had come to creating a brand association was during its 1998 Super Bowl run—before Michael Vick—in which running back Jamal Anderson created a dance in the end zone called the "Dirty Bird." Although it appealed to some segments of the Falcons fan base, it quickly faded when Anderson suffered a season-ending injury the following year and the Falcons returned to mediocrity.

Things had to change. Team owner Arthur Blank was a proven businessman and would apply a businesslike approach to change the brand's trajectory. As the founder and former CEO of the Home Depot, Blank was a visionary who had revolutionized the home improvement retail business. He would now need to provide the vision to revitalize an on-the-field product and brand that was clearly in disarray.

While Blank would begin the transformation of the operational side of the Falcons by bringing in a new general manager and head coach, he would task Jim Smith and his marketing team to rebuild the Falcons brand. "For all the negativity that occurred out of the Vick and Petrino situations," Smith said, "there clearly was an upside. It enabled us to begin to build a foundation. It enabled us to relook at our brand and understand that what we had been doing for the previous forty-plus years wasn't working. It enabled us to start redefining our *relationship* with our fans."

Smith's first task was to *identify* the Falcons fan base. Until now, little, if any, marketing research to understand fans' perception of the team had been conducted. According to Smith, "It wasn't like we were Coca-Cola or Budweiser. We had a small staff, limited budget, and really didn't have the ability to understand who our fan base was, much less what they wanted." That was about to change.

Smith hunkered down with his marketing team and emerged with a hypothesis: *Clubs can improve their relationships with fans without having to rely on consistent success on the field.* In theory, this sounded great: no longer would the Falcons brand live and die by the results on the field. Smith put it this way: "Don't get me wrong, the on-the-field performance is huge, and it makes our job much easier when the team is successful. But we just couldn't be trapped by the expectation that our brand would be strong only if the team won. NFL clubs can't control wins and losses, but they can influence all of the other experiences with their fans. If you look at the NFL clubs with strong national brands, they have built team traditions and identities that focus on the fan."

First, Smith needed to test this hypothesis. He and his team had to understand and articulate who the Falcons fans were and why they were fans. What had the Falcons done to attract these fans, and, more important, what did they need to do to cement this relationship and engage more fans?

Around the same time, the NFL was developing a comprehensive tracking system to better understand its fan base and measure fans' reaction to their game-day experience. It needed a "guinea pig" for the study. The Falcons were one of two teams to sign up.

The Falcons Fan

When combined with internal Falcons ticket-holder data, the research revealed some interesting dynamics. First, the team discovered that the Falcons fan base was quite diverse (see Table 8.1).

Demographically, their fan base was all over the map. Women made up 45 percent of the fan base. There were a significant percentage of African Americans. The age range was broad. In fact, there wasn't one core type of fan that the Falcons could focus on like a laser. How would they be able to revitalize a brand to engage such a diverse group of individuals?

The next problem was the Atlanta market as a whole. It was a weak pro football market on a number of measures.

Table 8.1 Falcons Fan Demographics

	Falcons Fans (in Atlanta) (%)
Male	55
Female	45
Ages 25–54	56
Annual income > $75,000	47
Own residence	79
Caucasian	66
African American	30

Sources: 2008–2010 TNS/ESPN Sports Poll, Atlanta Falcons market report, and Falcons internal data.

Consider TV viewing, which is responsible for more than half of a team's revenues. With Michael Vick gone for the 2007 season, Atlanta had ranked twenty-ninth out of thirty-two NFL teams in NFL TV viewing. Four decades of losing seasons, the Vick suspension, and general team dysfunction had caused a decline in interest from the fan base.

Data comparing Atlanta's fan base with the total U.S. fan base did not paint a pretty picture either. On the basis of answers to specific questions, fans were categorized as avid (very interested in the NFL), casual (somewhat interested), or light/non fans (little bit/not at all interested); see Table 8.2.

The Falcons fan base was decidedly more "casual" compared with the total U.S. NFL fan base. This clearly explained why fans were leaving in droves in the wake of the Vick scandal. The Falcon brand hadn't established a strong enough relationship with its consumer base to keep fans engaged in tough times. The question was, why? Certainly the history of

Table 8.2 Football Fan Interest Level: Atlanta vs. National

	U.S. Population (%)	Atlanta Market (%)
Avid	34	28
Casual	23	32
Light/Non Fan	43	40

Sources: 2008–2010 TNS/ESPN Sports Poll, Atlanta Falcons market report, and Falcons internal data.

Table 8.3 Top Five Sports: Atlanta vs. National

	U.S. Population (%)	Atlanta Market (%)
NFL	23	17
MLB	11	11
College football	10	21
NBA	7	3
College basketball	4	N/A
NASCAR	N/A	3

Sources: 2008–2010 TNS/ESPN Sports Poll, Atlanta Falcons market report, and Falcons internal data.

losing seasons didn't help. But were there other drivers of fan enthusiasm that were causing this? The data revealed some interesting reasons. In the same NFL-sponsored fan tracking system, fans were asked to name their favorite spectator sport (Table 8.3).

What became clear was that college, not professional, football dominated the Atlanta market. In fact, more than *twice* the percentage of Atlantans said college football was their favorite sport compared to the national average. With two consistent college football powers in Georgia Tech (downtown Atlanta) and the University of Georgia (seventy miles away in Athens), plus another seven major college football programs within a four-hour drive, college football trumped the NFL. Given that its geographical location was in the heart of both Southeastern Conference (SEC) and Atlantic Coast Conference (ACC) country, Atlanta was a college football mecca. Atlanta football fans were spending Saturdays watching college football either live or in person. That left Sundays for errands, family time, and other recreational activities. If football had to be missed for other activities, it wasn't going to be the Georgia-Florida game. It was going to be the Falcons.

Furthermore, the Atlanta market was a city of "transplants." As the capital of the "New South," Atlanta had grown significantly in population, from 2.3 million in 1981 to 5.5 million when Michael Vick entered the federal penitentiary. Only 40 percent of those who lived in the metro Atlanta area were born in Georgia. This was the lowest number of any of the top twenty metropolitan areas. Other cities had significant populations that lived their whole lives in the same location; Atlanta was an anomaly. In fact, for many NFL fans who lived in Atlanta, the Falcons were their second-favorite team, their favorite being their hometown team. That would be difficult to change.

The other challenge the Falcons faced was the large number of options available for the entertainment dollar in the Atlanta market. The city had a sports franchise in every league, college football reigned supreme, and concert and Broadway entertainment rivaled almost any other city. In addition, moderate weather encouraged lots of outdoor activities: golf, tennis, boating, hiking in the North Georgia mountains, and amusement parks.

While the team wrestled with the challenges of attracting fans, it also faced the larger conundrum: What *was* the Falcons brand? Research indicated that the Falcons did own "that one thing"—it was just not something they wanted or needed to own anymore. In a word-association exercise, when asked the first word that came to mind when thinking about the Atlanta Falcons, an overwhelming majority of fans answered "Michael Vick." The second most common word was "Dirty Birds," that tired moniker from the lone Super Bowl team ten years prior. Nothing else registered. In essence, the Falcons brand boiled down to a guy who had pleaded guilty to killing dogs and a ten-year-old end-zone dance.

This is what the Atlanta Falcons marketing team faced in December 2007. Fans were betrayed, the forty-second season had come and gone without consecutive winning seasons, and the marketing team was trying to prove that they could develop a brand without a guarantee that the team it was marketing would ever win consistently. But they were convinced that they could pull it off. The reason? They were heartened by one piece of data from the NFL team market research that identified the most popular NFL team in the United States. It wasn't just the most popular NFL team but the most popular sports franchise in the country. It had been valued at over $1.65 billion by *Forbes*.[3] However, since 1996, this team had won a grand total of *one* playoff football game. The Falcons, in contrast, had won four playoff games since 1996 and had appeared in a Super Bowl and two NFC Championship games.

The Dallas Cowboys were the most popular and highest-valued team in the NFL. The Cowboys had the history—five Super Bowl titles. But they had done nothing of note on the field since a Super Bowl win over the Pittsburgh Steelers in 1995. The difference was that the Cowboys had built a brand. They had a created a strong relationship with their fan base, built on a long-standing tradition that dated back to the team's origins in the 1960s. Although some of the brand's foundation had been built by the club's success in the 1970s through 1995, much of it had been built off the field. The unique experience of Texas Stadium and now Cowboys Stadium, with their holes in the roof; the Dallas Cowboys Cheerleaders; the Dallas Cowboys Ring of Honor; the built-up rivalries with fellow division teams the Washington Redskins, Philadelphia Eagles, and New York Giants; and the classic Cowboys lone-star logo—all created a brand that went well beyond the field of play. The relationship between the Cowboys and their fans was so strong that *no matter how the team did on the field, it would still remain the most popular and ultimately the most valuable brand franchise in all of sports.*

Rebuilding the Brand

The Falcons marketing team began to explore what the Falcons brand should be. The goal was simple: the Falcons had to increase the number of "avid" fans, pulling from the larger "casual" fan bucket. They had to create or reestablish a closer relationship with the fan base. The relationship had to be one in which fans actually cared about the team, its players, and its future. When it came to the myriad choices in sports and entertainment in Atlanta, they would not just passively accept the team but *choose* to actively be a part of the Falcons family.

To bring about this change, the Falcons would have to decide what their brand stood for, and ensure that it was properly and consistently communicated every time the brand "spoke" to its fan base. Everything would communicate and every communication would be consistent. What else would the Falcons need to do to generate more passion? Jim Smith and his team had to determine how the Falcons were unique, compared not just to other football teams but to all the other sports and entertainment options that beckoned the Atlanta consumer.

The Falcons marketing team analyzed fan research, talked with players and management, and conducted internal brainstorming sessions to deliver the following six values that represented the post–Michael Vick/Bobby Petrino disaster. They would define who the Falcons were, and they would serve as the foundation of the brand. In fact, these six values would serve as the foundation for a movement.

Unity. *Together as a team, as a single unit with a single purpose, we can go wherever we dare to dream. We build unity and cohesion, pulling people together behind our club.*

No longer would the Falcons hang their banner around the neck of one player. The Falcons, in both their on-the-field performance and off-the field relationship with fans, would emphasize the team rather than the individual. The emotional, timeless qualities of unity, cohesion, and teamwork would be an integral part of the Falcons brand.

Power. *We are stronger. We have greater desire. We cannot be stopped. We are a powerful force in the National Football League.*

Power was a lynchpin of football in the South and served as a foundation for success. The coaching staff was developing a team that would run a conservative offense built on a strong and powerful running game, short passes, and a dominant defense, instead of a high-scoring team that relied on trick plays and gimmicky passes. The idea of power fit perfectly as a core brand idea both on and off the field.

Youth. *We are young, and we are hungry. We bring fresh thinking and dynamism to everything we do.*

The on-the-field Falcons would feature young, up-and-coming players like quarterback Matt Ryan and wide receiver Roddy White, and would continue to bring on young new talent. But this value would go beyond the players. The Falcons as an organization would be innovative and different in how they conducted themselves in their relationships with fans, exceeding what was typical and surpassing all expectations.

Integrity. *We will take the righteous road. We will work harder. We know that there are no shortcuts to success. We will operate to the highest standards in the National Football League.*

Given the issues with Vick, this was a must. The Falcons had to ensure that they built a perception of a team that had honor, decency, and integrity–both on and off the field. The damage that the Vick incident had done to the entire organization could not be underestimated. The Falcons would need to overdeliver on this value and convince their fan base that the Vick incident did not reflect the team's values.

Community. Every time we put on that Falcons jersey, we are playing for more than just ourselves. We will draw our strength from the community we serve, and we will give back to that community to make it stronger.

To appeal to Atlantans beyond wins and losses, the Falcons were going to have to play a significant role within the community. Visits, camps, meet-and-greets with fans, and clinics would be a major push of the Falcons marketing plan. The Falcons would establish an ongoing relationship that transcended Sunday afternoons. It was imperative to be seen as an asset to the community.

Modern South. We are the new breed. We are a new energy. We are proud of our origins.

The Falcons were going to acknowledge their southern origins in a unique way that truly represented the New South. Atlanta was the capital of the modern South—busy, international, progressive, and accommodating—and the Falcons would likewise be a team for all of Atlanta. Even if a fan hailed from Pittsburgh, Miami, or Chicago, the Falcons would create a brand with which the many transplants in the city would be able to engage. The Falcons would develop a relationship with fans by celebrating the city they were proud to represent.

The marketing team then took these key values and came up with "the Falcons Brand Mantra." It was encapsulated in a few short phrases. *Everything* that would be presented to the fans in the context of their relationship with the Falcons would stem from this brand essence. It would drive the advertising, the promotion, and the website—every consumer touchpoint.

The Atlanta Falcons are
Authentic
> With a rich and deep-rooted history in Atlanta, we are the number-one team of the South.

Magnetic
> We attract and unite the most diverse group of fans.

Elevating
> We are uplifting. Every experience with the Atlanta Falcons is electric.

Creating a Movement

The Falcons' ultimate goal would be to hear a fan, when asked to describe the Atlanta Falcons, say: "The Atlanta Falcons Raise Me Up!" Across every touchpoint with fans, the Falcons would communicate this core idea. From their reintroduction to casual fans to their ongoing dialogue with longtime avid fans, the Falcons would communicate the core values. Smith says, "We weren't going to create a campaign. We were going to create a movement. It was the only way we could rise up from the disappointments of the past." It would become the team's new personality. No Jerry Glanville or Michael Vick. The Falcons were moving away from their gimmicky past.

The right message to a skeptical fan base would be critical. After working on multiple iterations, the team came up with one that worked on many levels: "Atlanta Falcons—Rise Up." It was short and pithy, and communicated significant meaning. It addressed the Falcons' recent struggles, yet provided imagery of another bird, a phoenix, rising from the ashes and becoming whole again.

To communicate the new message, the Falcons needed a spokesman who was passionate, could rally the fans, and could also be seen as a credible representative of the team. Just as smartwater found in Jennifer Aniston a spokesperson who accurately represented the brand's personality, the Falcons needed someone to embody the redesigned Falcons brand. In their search, they discovered someone who had Atlanta ties, had attended nearby Morehouse College, and had sold concessions at the team's previous home, old Fulton County Stadium. It didn't hurt that at the time, he was the highest-grossing actor in Hollywood. After some convincing by Smith and his team, Samuel Jackson agreed to become the face of the Falcon's "Rise Up" campaign.

The remade Falcons brand would now have an opportunity to reintroduce the team to a fan base starved for some positive news. The "Rise Up" ad alternated scenes of the Falcons making key plays, the crowd cheering in the Georgia dome, Jackson clad in a black suit and bright red tie, and a multicultural choir in red robes singing in the background. Optimistic and inspirational, the ad offered a modern-day version of a traditional Sunday sermon with the choir in the background and Jackson resembling an old-time minister. Smith says, "'Rise Up' would become a motivational cry for the city, the community, and in the stadium."[4] What is interesting is not just what is in the spot but what is *not* in the spot.

First, there is no mention of specific players. Although visuals were shown of current QB Matt Ryan and others, none were mentioned by name. In fact, out of the entire one-minute ad, less than twenty seconds featured players on the field. One could argue that the fans cheering in the Dome, and the experience itself, were featured as much as the players on the field. This ad campaign would have players and action, but they would be *in the background*. The Falcons would be bigger than what was going on in the field. No discussion around wins or losses, but instead an inspirational message that would appeal to every fan's emotions.

The spot did exactly what Jim Smith hoped it would do. It began to control the uncontrollable. He says, "The 'Rise Up' campaign really put in motion that we were something new and different. We were, if you will, rising up from where we had been, from that awful time, and we were in a new space. You were going to see a new Falcons team, a new management style, and it was something to be hopeful about."

The movement began. Every time the team interacted with its fan base, "Rise Up" would be central to the conversation. In fact, every time the Falcons brand came into contact with consumers, the goal was consistency in message. It wasn't limited to Sunday afternoons at the Dome or on TV, but was aimed at growing the fan relationship on an ongoing basis. The website was revamped to include an array of videos featuring Falcons players, coaches, and management involved in a variety of activities that allowed fans to get to know the team beyond the three-hour game on Sundays.

Of course, their product was that three-hour game, and the in-stadium entertainment experience had to deliver. Smith and his team made drastic changes to what had deflated into a relatively lifeless in-game experience. It wasn't an easy task. First, they focused on surroundings. The video displays had to be changed. The Falcons had the smallest video board in the NFL. Fans wanted visual enhancements to the in-game experience, such as videos and replays, and the Falcons weren't delivering. So the team undertook a massive effort to create some of the largest video boards in any NFL stadium. The boards became a primary focus of the game-day experience. Not surprisingly, the Jackson "Rise Up" spots were shown at the start and during key points of the game to rally the fans to "Rise Up" and cheer for the team. The in-stadium experience also included fireworks, dancing, and entertainment to appeal across the various demographics, all linking back to the "Rise Up" idea.

Ultimately, "Rise Up" went way beyond the Atlanta Falcons. It did ultimately become a movement. It became part of the community. "Rise Up" started representing the city of Atlanta as a whole. It became a source of community pride and even volunteerism. For example, a community volunteering website, www.riseupatlanta.com, was created that let fans join the Atlanta Falcons in helping make Atlanta better—one day, one hour, one volunteer event at a time.

Locally, this made an impact. Fan research proved this out. Figure 8.1 shows a word cloud that depicts the team's reputation nationally. The size of the word indicates the relative number of mentions when consumers are asked to describe the Falcons brand. Nationally, you'll see that Michael Vick was still the prominent association, with the "Dirty Birds" dance second. Now compare it to Figure 8.2, a

Figure 8.1 Falcons Fan Perceptions, National (2009)

Figure 8.2 Falcons Fan Perceptions, Atlanta (2009)

word cloud of brand perceptions by fans in the Atlanta market one year into the "Rise Up" campaign (2009). Large words in the Atlanta word cloud include, in addition to prominent team owner Arthur Blank, words like "team," "commitment," "exciting," and "community."

Had the brand been completely revitalized? Of course not. There were still words (such as "inconsistent") that would take time to change. But Jim Smith and his team liked what they were seeing. The numbers were improving. The Falcons had gone from twenty-ninth to twenty-second in fan commitment out of thirty-two teams. They improved to being the twentieth-favorite football team in America. An additional 5 percent of "casual" fans were evolving into "avid" fans. It wasn't happening overnight. When brands undergo crises in their relationship with consumers, rebuilding that relationship takes much longer than dismantling it, but the marketing team saw improvement. The momentum was there. It would be further aided by an agreement between the Falcons and the city of Atlanta to build a new Falcons stadium. Smith and his team would now be able to impact the fan experience even more directly with input into the new stadium's design and features.

MANAGING THROUGH CRISIS

What can we take away from the story of the Atlanta Falcons? It shows that building brand-consumer relationships isn't easy. It takes time. It takes patience. And all that work can come undone with one crisis. How should marketers respond to a brand crisis?

- *Ask yourself: Is there really a problem?* Given the confluence of events that hit the Falcons, it was relatively easy to determine that there was a problem. But brand crises are rarely that cut and dried. Judgment is critical in determining whether a problem really exists. The last thing a marketer wants to do is sound alarms and invest time and resources for a nonexistent problem. At Coke, we used the rule of three: if we heard from three different sources about a potential issue, we took it seriously. Marketers need to define their rule for action prior to a crisis and be able to judge confidently and decisively whether a problem is significant enough to be addressed.

- *Create an action plan.* Once the problem was identified, Jim Smith and his Falcons team developed a process to right the brand relationship. It involved taking inventory of the situation, engaging outside help (the NFL), conducting research to understand the extent of the problem, and using the insights from that research to craft a comprehensive road map to brand revitalization.

Depending on the situation, action plans can range from simply monitoring a situation to a total product recall or change. But, by its very nature, it involves *action*. As soon as an issue is discovered, the marketer must be proactive in assembling a team that will be responsible for outlining potential consequences and the outcomes of various options in solving the crisis. Similar to the way the Falcons handled the Vick-Petrino crisis, an effective action plan will set objectives to be met and specify strategies for achieving those objectives.

- *Be up-front.* Throughout the Vick-Petrino crisis, Falcons management was lauded for their transparency with fans regarding the actions they would be pursuing. There is a powerful lesson here. With senior management, partners, and especially consumers, be open and transparent about the crisis. Admit the issue and outline the steps being put in place to correct it. The traditional mantra in regard to well-publicized political, business, sports, or entertainment scandals is that it's not the original sin that brings one down, it's the attempted cover-up. Consumers are impatient and will move on to another competitor as soon as they feel that their trust in a brand has been broken. If it has been broken, it must be repaired quickly.

- *Leverage the crisis to strengthen the brand's relationship with the consumer.* Although a brand-consumer crisis can be arduous to maneuver through, there is potential for an upside. Just as the Falcons used the Vick and Petrino incidents as a restart with consumers, a proactive, truthful, and engaging response to any brand crisis may not just solve the issue at hand but also give the relationship a much-needed jolt and reconnect the brand and consumer more closely.

"Rise Up" provided a multidimensional way to connect with the consumer. There was, of course, the idea of rising up from the past and the idea of rising up during the game, but "Rise Up" meant something more, too. "Rise Up" could be a movement and could be used personally. How did the Falcons fans "Rise Up" in their own lives? "Rise Up" became a statement and established that emotional connection with the Falcons fan.

- *Make the relationship your top priority.* The Falcons had one goal: they were not going to let one player and one coach bring down an entire franchise. The Falcons could have tried to cover up the incident; they could have acted more in the self-interest of Vick, Petrino, or the franchise, but they didn't. The relationship with the fan base became the priority. As has been documented throughout this book, maintaining and enhancing the relationship between brand and consumer must take precedence over any short-term volume or profit hit. An immediate investment will be well worth the time, cost, and effort if that relationship is saved.

• • •

A crisis is often a turning point in the brand-consumer relationship. How it is handled will either give the brand the opportunity to reengage more powerfully with consumers or result in the ending of the relationship. In the Falcons case, the brand emerged from the crisis stronger than ever. But what about those brand-consumer relationships where the end *slowly* comes into sight? How does one realize that changes are required for the betterment of both the brand and the consumer?

When signs start to emerge that something is not right with the brand-consumer relationship, any decision entails a tremendous amount of risk because usually something has to be done before the problems are 100 percent obvious. The marketer is faced with a challenging question: Does the situation require doing something completely different, which carries the risk that the effort may fail, or is doing nothing the bigger risk, as it may result in a decline that only accelerates? It takes a special marketer to be able to recognize that something is wrong. It is even more challenging to make a compelling recommendation of the proper action. In the next chapter, we'll look at the end of a relationship—how both brands and consumers realize it's over, and, more important, what to do when that happens.

9

BREAKING UP AND MOVING ON

Just like our relationships with people, brand-consumer relationships can deteriorate. Boredom, dissatisfaction, and lack of communication all are signs of a relationship going bad. When your brand's relationship with its consumers declines, you have three choices: (1) rescue the relationship with the existing consumer base, (2) focus your efforts on forming a stronger bond with a different consumer group so that the brand can continue to thrive, or (3) make the tough decision that the brand is no longer relevant and should be discontinued. We discussed option 1 in Chapter Eight, and in this chapter, we'll discuss the other two. Determining that the relationship is in trouble is the first step for any marketer. Too often marketers misread the cues.

THE SOUR TASTE OF "LYMON"

Darryl Cobbin did not miss the cues. In the summer of 1991, as a newly minted MBA who had just accepted a job as an assistant brand manager at The Coca-Cola Company, he had one objective: to be assigned to the Sprite brand. If you were to look at where Sprite was at the time, you'd have to ask yourself why he was so enthusiastic about the brand. At the time, Sprite was a midsize soft drink brand that was being dominated in the lemon-lime category by 7UP, which was roughly three times larger. Sprite was a brand that was static, bordering on a decline. It had experienced zero or negative growth for nearly a decade. It wasn't as though Sprite was marketing to a group of individuals to whom Cobbin, as a twenty-seven-year-old African American male, felt that he could strongly relate. Sprite's consumer base (I won't even call them influencers) comprised what Coke called Home Category Managers (HCMs), what you and I would refer to as "moms," who were thirty-four and over. The HCMs received the bulk of Sprite's attention.

So why did Cobbin want Sprite? Well, he had seen a Sprite commercial on BET designed for the African American consumer market (AACM) that featured an early hip-hop group at the time, Heavy D and The Boys. In addition to the designated brand team, Coca-Cola had a separate marketing group that developed messaging for specific consumer groups, such as African Americans, Hispanics, and blue-collar consumers, for some of the company's major brands. This was a campaign that originated from the AACM group, but Cobbin realized that it was pushing the envelope for a relatively conservative company like Coke. The Sprite media buy against AACM was simply that—a media buy—probably less than 5 percent of the total budget, but Cobbin explains, "I thought to myself, if a company that size is willing to try this, there might be more freedom on this brand than Coca-Cola, where the brand manager is really the CEO."[1]

Cobbin must have impressed the brass at Coke, because they granted him his wish. As he started his new job on Sprite, he discovered that there was an air of excitement around the building for the brand. A deal had just been completed with an upcoming movie and its lead actor that would create an association that was thought to be perfect for Sprite and its ongoing quest to win over HCMs. The hope was that it would reinvigorate the brand and put Sprite's romance with moms and the family back on track.

The movie that Sprite was pinning its hopes on to rekindle its relationship with its core consumer base was *Home Alone 2*, and the actor they would use was Macaulay Caulkin. This was a big, bold move for Sprite in 1991. It was the first major association of its kind for the brand. Sprite had never used celebrities before. Its messaging focused on the functional benefits of the great "Lymon" taste of Sprite that enabled people to express themselves (an emotional benefit) in unexpected ways. Great things were expected from this tie-in.

Unfortunately, great things did not manifest. The brand remained stagnant. It wasn't experiencing a nosedive, mind you, but it just wasn't growing like a brand should with the kind of marketing that was being put behind it.

As the *Home Alone 2* debacle was occurring, Cobbin was doing what most assistant brand managers do—trying to understand the business and get his bearings around a very large Coca-Cola organization. He quickly realized that Coca-Cola was a strongly data-driven organization, and unless a strategy could be backed up, it wouldn't fly. His manager, Steve Horn, who headed up the marketing for Coke's citrus brands, including Sprite, Mello Yello, and Fresca, asked Cobbin to dig deep and develop a story as to why the brand wasn't responding better.

As he analyzed the data, Cobbin found something intriguing. First, even though Sprite was not growing at the national level, when he looked at zip codes, he found that the brand *was* growing in certain areas. Interestingly, Sprite was doing well in areas that had a high percentage of African American and Hispanic consumers. Even in Los Angeles, the number-one 7UP market in the country (but a market with a high percentage of Hispanics), Sprite was growing. Looking further, he saw that the growth was being driven by young males. There appeared to be something connecting between Sprite and urban teen males. A company-wide consumer tracking study showed that compared to their Caucasian counterparts, a higher percentage of African Americans said that Sprite was their favorite brand.

Now this phenomenon wasn't just happening with Sprite; it was going on throughout the soft drink category. The young male demographic was also driving the volume of the two fastest-growing soft drink brands, Mountain Dew and Dr Pepper. While these two brands were focusing their efforts on young males, Sprite was trying to appeal to HCMs, a group that was not involved in this volume explosion.

Cobbin's analysis led him to one conclusion. If young males were driving the soft drink category's growth and young males of color were the one group that was growing in the Sprite consumer franchise, Macaulay Caulkin, *Home Alone 2*, and HCMs weren't going to do it. A new primary consumer relationship was needed.

Cobbin presented his findings to Steve Horn. Horn found them intriguing and encouraged the Sprite team to talk to a variety of consumers, including teen males and females as well as HCMs to find out more about the state of each consumer's relationship with the brand. This would then be compared to these consumers' relationship with Mountain Dew and Dr Pepper.

The Sprite 5 Cs

The research was executed, and the findings were remarkable. Consumers of all types had a clear, consistent perception of Mountain Dew and Dr Pepper. Mountain Dew was all about adrenaline, caffeine, action sports, and young guys, and had a smooth, citrus taste. Dr Pepper was all about individuality and accepting your uniqueness, and had a spicy, distinctive taste.

In contrast, Sprite was perceived in a variety of ways, depending on whom you talked to. HCMs saw Sprite as cute, funny, and friendly, and its taste was crisp, clean, clear, and cool. Teen males and females both said that they really didn't understand what Sprite was about, but what they did see, they didn't like. They weren't into the Sprite commercials that featured guys having water fights, playing with monkeys at a zoo, and making faces at someone when the person was turning his or her head. Teen males thought this was stupid. But when teens were asked about the Sprite product itself, they said the *exact* same things that the HCMs had said. Sprite was crisp, clean, clear, and cool—all positive. Cobbin concluded that

"Sprite didn't have a product problem. Sprite had a brand problem."

He explains, "I saw that the only thing that we had that was positive were those four product attributes, the four Cs." (Later a fifth C, caffeine free, would be added.) He says, "Why not take those descriptors of Sprite and turn them into emotional benefits that would attract that young male consumer?" Teen males were driving category growth. Dr Pepper and Mountain Dew had figured it out and were talking to them. Sprite hadn't been, but would now start. The brand would "break up" with and walk away from its stable but static consumer base of HCMs and instead focus its marketing efforts on the important teen urban male consumer.

But how would they align the brand's five Cs with the attitude that was needed to attract African American and Hispanic young males? Cobbin had an answer. There was a small but growing movement in large metropolitan areas known as hip-hop. A few artists had broken through with a couple of hits. Most of society thought that these were just a couple of hit "rap" records. But Cobbin knew more. As a native of inner-city Detroit, he was well tuned in to what was progressing in the African American community in urban areas. He knew that there was an entire subculture from which this music emerged. The culture included not only rappers but also artists, dancers, and DJs. In short, within the African American community, hip-hop was gaining such momentum that it had the potential to be massive in terms of cultural influence. Hip-hop would represent the Sprite influencer, and Cobbin would use it as a foundation to communicate Sprite's five Cs.

Using his own knowledge as well as insights from young male hip-hop artists, Cobbin and the Sprite team aligned the Sprite five Cs with hip-hop:

1. *Crisp*—represents the sharp dress that was part of the hip-hop scene: the hat, shirt, and shoes.
2. *Clean*—a reference to an overall look. "I'm so clean and look so good that you can't touch me."
3. *Caffeine free*—no hype or "BS." "I don't need to add anything. I am good the way I am."
4. *Clear*—again, no BS; there aren't any filters here. "I am the real deal."

All of these added up to number 5, *Cool*. It wasn't necessarily about being on the football team. Within the hip-hop context, cool equaled confidence. From a teen male's perspective, it was "doing what I think is right for me and having the confidence to know that I am going to be OK."

From these five Cs, the Sprite team laddered up to a brand essence that would represent Sprite in its new communication with consumers. It would be the crux of a new relationship with a new influencer group, young urban males. Gone would be the great "Lymon" taste of Sprite communicated to HCMs. Instead there would be a dramatically different positioning that would boil down to a three-word brand essence: "Trust Your Instincts."

The team began planning how the brand would go to market. Recall that 7UP was three times larger than Sprite. Well, citrus director Steve Horn decided that the brand's main competitor shouldn't be 7UP. Horn believed that when a male teen went into a store to get a beverage, he didn't say, "I think I'm in the mood for a citrus-flavor soft drink, or I feel like a cherry cola." What Horn believed was that teens went into stores looking for something that tasted good. So the team aimed higher than just 7UP. Their goal would be to take volume away from any soft drink volume. Sprite would start playing offense and going after the volume of the big category brands.

The Sprite team went to Coke management with the new positioning and strategy. It was a big risk. The idea hadn't been proven or tested. The brand team was relying on Cobbin's original volume analysis, the qualitative work comparing Sprite with Mountain Dew and Dr Pepper, and a new advertising strategy. Nevertheless, Coke management saw promise and agreed to test it, but purposely did not give the brand any more resources than it had the prior year. If the new positioning was going to succeed, it would have to succeed on its own merits. It would not be getting additional support from the company.

Sprite's goal was to become the fastest-growing soft drink in the industry. For a brand that hadn't grown in eight years, this was a tall order. But the team believed that by executing a three-part strategy over multiple years, they could achieve that goal. The strategy was straightforward:

- A compelling positioning and communication
- Precise execution in retail stores through a meaningful brand association
- Consumer promotions that would drive consumption frequency

All three of these couldn't be implemented in the first year. In fact, the brand had the resources only to execute the first plank, a new consumer positioning and message.

"Obey Your Thirst" Communication

The advertising agency Lowe Lintas would take the "Trust Your Instincts" positioning idea and articulate it in a way that would appeal to the young urban male. It came back with a tagline that would serve as an invitation to young males to engage with the brand. The ending message would simply say "Image Is Nothing. Thirst Is Everything. Obey Your Thirst." Cobbin says, "In short, what we were saying was this: 'Look, you're smart and you see through the BS that is out there. You have your own life to lead, and no one is going to tell you how to act or what to do. And oh, by the way, if you do get thirsty, pick up a Sprite, but only if you want to.' In 1994, that was a radically different message."

The advertising itself would also be groundbreaking. Sprite's general-market, mainstream advertising would now have an urban tone to it. It would be edgy. It would be bold. It would also have an African American teen male narrating. Cobbin notes that, although it feels like recent history, he could not recall any mainstream brand at the time that had an African American teen narrating its commercials. Maybe the ones meant for BET, but certainly not for the general market.

Meanwhile, the African American media buys would become a much larger percentage of the overall budget. For these, the brand's multicultural agency, Burrell, led by Stanley Yorker and Reginald Jolly, created an edgy spot that featured several hip-hop artists who they felt best represented the hip-hop culture. Teen males who were aware of hip-hop certainly took notice. They knew hip-hop, and they knew that what Sprite was doing was very progressive, almost unheard of. At the same time, general-market teens weren't exactly sure what Sprite was doing, because they weren't up on hip-hop, but what they saw was cool. The approach that Sprite was using in its communication was known as layering: those in the know would understand exactly what the brand was communicating and be appreciative of it; those who weren't into hip-hop would think it was cool, but would have to work to discover what hip-hop actually was.

Then something even more intriguing happened. The media strategy changed even more abruptly. The brand team began to interchange the general-market spot and the African American spot between general-market and African American programming: the general-market "Image Is Nothing" campaign would run on African American programming, and the Burrell "Hip-Hop" advertising was shown on general-market TV. Urban teens really started noticing this. They knew that Sprite was making a deliberate attempt to reach out to them. A brand that they had dismissed as silly and stupid just a year ago was now seeking them out.

A Meaningful Association

With exactly the same budget as the prior year and with only the change in brand communication, Sprite, which as noted hadn't grown in eight years, grew at a robust 8.9 percent for the year. The new Sprite identity was starting to resonate. Coke management got behind the brand and gave the team carte blanche to continue to build a relationship with this new consumer group.

The brand needed additional support at retail stores in the form of in-store displays and promotions. A strong message was a start, but volume growth couldn't be fully realized without a strong presence in grocery stores, mass merchandisers, and convenience stores. One of the ways that The Coca-Cola Company was able to secure additional retailer display activity was through its many associations and sponsorships. Sprite needed one.

Cobbin's colleague, Michael Guth, felt that the NBA might be an opportunity. Players were coming into the league with a distinctive hip-hop look, from long baggy shorts to a new street attitude. It could be a perfect association—a national property that was seeing dramatic growth in viewership and attendance. The only problem was that The Coca-Cola Classic brand was currently leveraging the NBA association as the official soft drink of the NBA. But the Sprite team felt that the NBA could benefit Sprite more than the NBA could benefit the Coca-Cola Classic brand.

John Konradt, the new citrus flavor director, was tasked with selling the Sprite NBA association to Coca-Cola management and its bottling system. He made one simple point. The Coca-Cola Company used properties to increase the presence and relevance of its brands. Konradt asked two questions: (1) Which was bigger, Coca-Cola Classic or the NBA? The answer was obviously Coca-Cola Classic; (2) Which was bigger, Sprite or the NBA? The answer was the NBA. Company management agreed. If The Coca-Cola Company was to stay true to its property strategy, then the NBA was a better fit for Sprite.

Steve Koonin, the leader of the Coca-Cola sports marketing group, was tasked with selling the idea to the NBA commissioner, David Stern. Koonin told Stern that the Coca-Cola brand, with all its various associations (the Olympics, the NFL, the NHL) had to spread its promotional calendar out so that each had only a small window of time in which they were aligned with Coke. He asked Stern to make a choice: Would the NBA like to be associated with Coke for one six-week promotion or aligned with Sprite for the entire year? The NBA agreed that Sprite should be its official soft drink. Sprite now had a relevant association that aligned closely with its overall brand proposition. Two of the original three planks for Sprite's ultimate success had been achieved.

Building Consumption Frequency

Despite its strong start with the new positioning, the Sprite brand suffered a lack of frequent drinkers in terms of the percentage of heavy users who made up the brand's consumer base. In fact, Sprite's percentage of frequent users, those who consumed multiple Sprites in a day, was the lowest in the entire industry. It was half that of Pepsi, one-third that of Coca-Cola Classic, and one-quarter of Diet Coke. These numbers were partially driven by the fact that the brand was only just now engaging with the most frequent soft drink users, young males. It also suffered because its counterpart, 7UP, had been telling consumers for years that lemon-lime soft drinks were for those occasions when you didn't want a cola. Talk about limiting your consumption! 7UP had trained consumers to think of lemon-lime soft drinks as a "once in a while" beverage. Sprite would now have to undo this perception.

The brand needed to come up with a way to encourage its frequent users to drink more Sprite, and looked to a consumer promotion to do so. At that time, soft drink promotions focused on grand prizes. Consumers would win large-scale prizes like trips to Disney World. The odds of winning were so low that consumers never won and never knew anyone who won. In fact, in the mind of the Sprite influencer, soft drink promotions with impossible-to-achieve prizes were the very thing that the brand had been railing against in its "Image Is Nothing. Thirst Is Everything" messaging. If Sprite went out with a big promotion with a grand prize, at best it would be seen as disingenuous; at worst it could alienate a substantial portion of its influencers. It would be the equivalent of cheating on the consumer. Still, the brand needed something to drive consumption frequency.

The idea that emerged would change the nature of soft drink promotions. Sprite would execute a promotion that had no grand prize. No trips to the Super Bowl or Hawaii or any other exotic location. Instead, the concept was simple. There would only be one prize: a free twenty-ounce Sprite. Free Sprite would be given out at an amazing rate. One in six bottles would win; if you drank enough Sprite, you would get a free Sprite. This harkened back to the clarity of the product: there was no BS to this promotion. You drank Sprite, you won. Period.

The promotion accomplished two things: first, it helped with the frequency of consumption. It got consumers into the mind-set that Sprite could be enjoyed with the frequency of any other soft drink. Second, it continued to reinforce the powerful Sprite "Trust Your Instincts" message. Sales of twenty-ounce Sprite increased over 30 percent as a result of this initiative.

In the coming years, the brand continued to build on the three planks, including the signing of NBA star Grant Hill, using teasers to preview new Sprite spots, and leveraging the "Dream Team" as part of Coke's overall Olympic sponsorship. The brand continued to embrace the hip-hop culture, showing young people how the artists created their craft and setting the stage for two rival hip-hop artists to reconcile, which ultimately sent a message about getting past our differences from one another. The results speak for themselves. Cobbin reports that Sprite became the favorite brand of teen males. Not their favorite soft drink brand. Not their favorite beverage brand. Sprite became their favorite *brand in any category*. The brand's annual volume of six hundred million cases in 1997 was double the volume at the start of the decade. The initiative was so groundbreaking and successful that in 2003, Matthew Grimm of *Advertising Age* named the campaign one of the five most important marketing campaigns of the last quarter century.[2]

THE ART OF ADAPTATION

The story of Sprite's repositioning should be an inspiration to any marketer. Brands can start over. They can break up with one consumer group and start a new relationship with a different one. It's difficult but far from impossible. Success came to Sprite for three key reasons.

Both the brand team and the company were willing to take a calculated risk. Recall how we discussed smart risk in Chapter Seven? A calculated risk still has the potential to fail, but you go in knowing that you've done your homework. The Sprite team took a smart risk, but it was still a huge one. There is no doubt that to take this on, Darryl Cobbin had to demonstrate the very coolness that was so prevalent in the Sprite message.

Think about what Cobbin was advocating. He was asking The Coca-Cola Company for permission for Sprite to "break up" with HCMs and start a relationship with a completely different group of individuals with a message that was 180 degrees from where the brand had been. This was not only a risk that Cobbin took personally; it represented one for The Coca-Cola Company as well. Think about what Coca-Cola did. It accepted a recommendation that would make dramatic changes to its third-largest brand, initially put forth by a twenty-something-year-old brand manager. The company could have cautiously taken the easy road and not implemented the team's suggestion, but it knew that no one understood the situation better than that brand team and trusted them to do what was in the best interest of the brand. To play off the Sprite message, the company trusted the Sprite team's instincts.

If you are going to make a change, go big. The Sprite team could have played it safe. They could have dipped their toe into the ocean of this new positioning. It would have been very easy to go out and test a spot here and there and see if it made an impact. Had they done this, they would have lost the entire holistic push and energy that was put behind the brand. Like other successful brands that we have discussed, they sought to understand their consumer. They got to know him on a personal level. They had the insights. They had developed a strategy that logically emerged from those insights. If any of the three key planks had been missing, the brand might not have seen as dramatic a success. Energy behind the project might have dissipated, and they would never have known the true impact that the initiative could have had. Instead, they went after it hard and were successful.

They gave lots of love to their new consumers. The Sprite team was enamored with their new consumers. They truly cared about their welfare and wanted to represent them, and they let them know it. They had to send a message to these new consumers that they were important to the brand. Cobbin recently confided to me that at one point he had written a "love letter" to the young people whom the brand sought to support and represent. Paraphrasing his letter, Cobbin told me what the team loved about the consumer and the brand.

> We loved to bring light and attention to a youth
> culture that wasn't getting recognition. We loved to
> attach our brand to things that showed young people
> that we respected them. We loved what the hip-hop
> culture was bringing to light. We loved and respected
> our position to be a beacon that led the way and
> showed that big brands can market to young people
> in an authentic way, by being bold and taking risks.
> And because of our love for them, they rewarded us
> back with their love. They told us, "You give us a
> message that we can believe in. We love what you
> stand for, and for that reason, you are our brand.
> We're with you."

By truly caring about its consumers, the brand looked out for their welfare. This did not go unnoticed by the consumers. The brand exuded authenticity because it really did care. Cobbin believes that the Sprite team created a new approach to marketing to young people in this country. It wasn't about preaching to them, and it wasn't about splash and sizzle. It was about understanding them and, more important, respecting them. That respect led to a brand that watched out for and supported its consumer base.

SHOULD I STAY OR SHOULD I GO?

The biggest challenge that marketers must inevitably face is determining what to do when a consumer relationship has deteriorated. Some relationships end abruptly, but usually they decline over time. Sometimes the relationship can be saved, as we have seen in the Sprite and Geritol examples. The brand and consumer undergo "counseling," and change happens. Sometimes the consumer must change. Other times, the brand must change. Or maybe both change a little, and the relationship begins anew. But sometimes the relationship has disintegrated so badly that all involved would be better off if it were to cease. The key then is to determine how to sever the relationship.

At what point do we choose not to invest more time, resources, or promotion into a particular brand? Perhaps the decision is easy: we have other priorities, the consumers are unprofitable, or we've lost consumer trust in our proposition. Obvious signposts that a relationship is in trouble include declining consumer measures (despite repeated investment), retailer or channel pushback and emphasis on competitive products, or having to increase spending just to keep the numbers stable. But actually pulling the plug is hard. Should the brand be discontinued? Should there be a farewell period, like a farewell tour of your favorite classic rock band? Or do you just quietly stop investing and let the brand slowly fade into oblivion? This is often a difficult quandary.

The successful Meda Consumer Healthcare (MCH) strategy of taking brands that have been neglected and "resurrecting" their relationship with consumers adds yet another wrinkle to the problem. There may be something in the back of your mind which whispers that if enough resources were put behind this brand or if a strategy were modified, it could still work.

It is interesting to use MCH as a guide and analyze how the company determines which brands *not* to invest in and characteristics of those brands. The same criteria might also be used to decide whether to save or reposition existing brands within a firm's portfolio. Jeffrey Cohen will tell you that MCH will not acquire and engage in a brand relationship if[3]

- *The financials are off and cannot be repaired.* If this is the case, there is no wiggle room to invest in trying to grow a relationship with the consumer.
- *The brand is in a category where the brand means very little in the overall consumer selection process.* As much as we don't like to admit this as marketing people, there are categories in which purchases are strictly product driven and brands mean very little. Why invest in something that offers little value in the grand scheme of things?
- *The brand equity is at a deficit.* If a brand has a negative reputation that will be either very difficult or impossible to repair, then developing a new brand may make more sense than saving or acquiring the old one. The brand must have

some type of positive halo and the potential to grow with the consumer.

- *Maintaining the relationship results in a loss of focus.* As firms continue to add brands, fewer and fewer resources in the form of time, people, and money are available for each brand. Inevitably, brands will get left out. If a brand can't be given the internal attention necessary to repair an ongoing relationship with the consumer, then it may be a wiser choice to discontinue the brand so that the resources can go toward those opportunities with bigger potential.

In addition, one must be relatively confident that the investment and ultimate changes that the brand will undergo will move the needle with consumers. Sometimes a brand is so entrenched in a certain space that no amount of investment and activity will be able to rescue it. Sometimes it is better to just start over.

If we want to really understand the challenges of pulling the plug on a relationship, there is no better example than what many believe to be the biggest marketing blunder of all time, New Coke.

THE MARKETING BLUNDER OF THE CENTURY?

Every marketer knows the story. On April 23, 1985, The Coca-Cola Company launched a new formulation of Coca-Cola to replace the existing formulation. The backlash became so strong and so intense that less than three months later, the company announced that it was bringing back the original formulation, renamed Coca-Cola Classic. Most people assume that when Coca-Cola Classic returned to the shelf in the middle of that summer, New Coke quickly and quietly went away.

Not so. For the next few years, The Coca-Cola Company made a strong and diligent effort to develop a relationship between New Coke and a segment of the cola consumer base. The marketing team had started making inroads with their efforts to rescue a consumer relationship, but then a critical decision was made to end it. This is the rarely heard story of New Coke and what happened to it after Coca-Cola Classic returned.

To fully understand the relationship between New Coke and its consumer, you have to know something about the circumstances behind its launch. To summarize, Pepsi had a sweeter formula than the original Coca-Cola and, through aggressive marketing, had cut significantly into Coca-Cola share and consumer preference measures in the early 1980s. The Pepsi Challenge, implemented across the country beginning in 1975, but ramped up in the early 1980s, was a blind taste test in which consumers would take a sip of Pepsi and a sip of Coke and indicate which one they preferred. The test was tailor-made for Pepsi. Pepsi is sweeter and "smoother" than Coke, and, in sip tests, the product that is sweeter and smoother generally wins. This may have nothing to do with what a drinker prefers after an entire glass.[4] Although sweeter and smoother products may taste better in a sip situation, often you find that individuals will tire of the taste after an entire serving. Pepsi wasn't asking people to drink an entire serving. It was asking them to take a sip. Pepsi was totaling up the numbers—in markets all across the United States and was publicizing and advertising these data to claim that it was winning the Pepsi Challenge.

At the same time, Pepsi was aggressively marketing the brand with heavy advertising featuring Michael Jackson and other topical celebrities, using such associations to build relationships, especially with young adults. Pepsi was asking Coke's consumer base to "cheat" on the beloved American icon—even for just a purchase or two—and a lot of Coke's consumers were willing to do so. Volume, share, and many key consumer measures were trending up for Pepsi and beginning to decline for Coke.[5] Pepsi's intense focus on winning the Cola Wars was beginning to work. Coke needed to fight back. So a decision was made to launch a reformulated version of Coke— New Coke—that would consistently beat Pepsi in blind taste tests.

For the first few weeks, this strategy worked. Sales figures from early launch cities showed an increase of 8 percent compared to the same period the year before.[6] New Coke ratcheted up the news and noise of the Cola Wars—and received a ton of press and impressions, later estimated at an incremental $1 billion.[7] Some have noted that at the time of its launch, New Coke was the most tried brand in consumer products history. But we all know what happened. Over the weeks, a backlash started and grew at such a pace that seventy-seven days later, Coca-Cola Classic was reintroduced with great fanfare, with its sales and other measures ultimately climbing well over its pre–New Coke launch numbers. Although the success of Coca-Cola Classic was embraced, it left a big elephant in the room: What should The Coca-Cola Company do with New Coke?

A Place for New Coke

Steve Hutcherson had just come to Coke as a recent graduate of the University of Georgia's Masters of Brand Management program. His first assignment, working for brand manager Paul Porwoll, was the New Coke brand. Hutcherson explains, "We had essentially misaligned the roles of each brand. Technically, New Coke, when launched as "Coke" that April, was the parent brand, and Coca-Cola Classic was now technically the line extension. That posed some major problems because we had a line extension that was significantly larger and more popular than the parent brand."

The company couldn't just take New Coke away. Even after Coca-Cola Classic returned, New Coke had a 2 percent share of the soft drink market. That might not seem like a lot to you, but at the time, 2 share points were worth nearly $1.5 billion in retail sales. It was enough volume that the theory was that if The Coca-Cola Company had delisted New Coke, those users would return to Pepsi, and Pepsi, not Coke, could end up being the leading U.S. soft drink. That couldn't happen.

It was decided that New Coke would remain and play a critical role in the now escalating Cola Wars. Coca-Cola Classic would stay out of the fray, but New Coke would go in and challenge Pepsi. Porwoll and the team were charged with clearly defining a new role and marketplace relationship for New Coke. It would serve as a tactical weapon to attack Pepsi with the specific mission to discredit and disarm the Pepsi Challenge. Coke knew that New Coke would beat Pepsi in a taste test. Internal research showed that whereas Pepsi beat the original Coca-Cola formula (now

Coca-Cola Classic) by a 53-47 margin, New Coke would beat Pepsi by a 55-45 margin.

Hutcherson explains,

> The company would have Pepsi in a catch-22 with this strategy. We could make the claim that Coke beat Pepsi in a taste test. We would never say New Coke, just Coke, since the brand technically was "Coke" and only used the "new" modifier during its introductory period. This immediately would start to diffuse the claim within Pepsi's taste challenge. The loyal Coca-Cola Classic drinker stayed out of the fray and continued to hear leadership claims for "their" Coke. Pepsi, on the other hand, couldn't say, "Wait! You're talking about New Coke!" Because if they did that, they just admitted that their flagship brand was beaten in a taste test by the most rejected product in human history!

Coke augmented this new taste test claim with an ad campaign for young adults that featured very early CGI graphics and a character named Max Headroom who would make fun of Pepsi and emphasize that Coke tasted better. Much of this effort was focused at the local market level—to defend against the "Challenge" but also to develop more relevant local consumer relationships and legitimacy for New Coke itself. As a result, the Pepsi Challenge was all but over. Ironically enough, it was New Coke that played a significant role in its undoing.

Despite that tactical success, in 1986, Hutcherson and his new superiors, directors David Clapp and Ron Aspergen, knew that if New Coke was to survive and complement the broader portfolio, it would have to create its own strategy and its own positioning, and engage in its own relationship with a new consumer group—remembering, of course, that the overall perception of the brand was still that it had been an unmitigated disaster. Few consumers wanted to have anything to do with it, and it can be argued that many who were drinking it were doing so by mistake, as the graphics just read "Coke." So, in 1987, Clapp and his team were given a corporate mandate to undertake comprehensive research to determine if there was anything that could be done to rescue New Coke and change its relationship with consumers, especially among Pepsi drinkers.

The first problem the team encountered was that whenever they asked consumers why they didn't drink New Coke, they got one answer: it tasted bad. The team knew that even though the taste was markedly different from Coke's, New Coke did not in fact taste bad. The taste tests proved it. But consumers didn't want to believe that something that had been so roundly rejected by the marketplace could *possibly* taste good; it just wasn't logical. The team had to find some way to get to a deeper reason why New Coke had been rejected so thoroughly. Hutcherson explains: "We had to take the taste issue off the table. So, in our qualitative interviews with consumers, we did our own very informal taste tests between Coke Classic, Pepsi, and New Coke. But regardless of what the consumer chose, we told them that they had picked New Coke! We had to do this so that they would go beyond the factual argument around taste issues that we knew didn't exist. We had to dig deeper to find some way to battle the logic of 'If I don't like this brand, it has to taste bad; otherwise, why would I not like it?'"

After putting aside the initial taste argument in this research, they asked again, "Why don't you like New Coke?" They received two interesting answers, one of which was conceptual and one that was relational. The conceptual response was that the consumers didn't know why Coke had done this to them in the first place: why take away or change America's most beloved product? It felt personal. Talk about cheating! The consumer was angry with The Coca-Cola Company, and New Coke was receiving the brunt of that anger. In the consumer's mind, Coke had never told him or her why it did what it did. The second response was more peer oriented or relational. New Coke had negative social benefits. No one they knew drank it. It was a laughingstock. They wouldn't be caught dead drinking it.

It was concluded that there were three barriers to sale of New Coke: (1) the seemingly logical argument that it somehow must taste bad, (2) the anger and confusion as to why The Coca-Cola Company came up with New Coke in the first place, and (3) the perception that no one was drinking it—that it was a loser brand for losers. Clapp's team of Hutcherson and some of the company's best marketing researchers (Jerry Payne and Barbara Ciesla) believed that if they were able to address barriers 2 and 3 successfully, the taste barrier would logically go away as well.

Repositioning New Coke

Coca-Cola would now play offense with New Coke, with the express desire to begin a relationship with Pepsi drinkers. In addition to the continuing taste-test challenge in select markets, a simple communication was developed. The spot, titled "Omnibus," opened by featuring a beautiful bottle of Coca-Cola (Classic) in the green contour bottle, icy cold. A voiceover introduced "Coca-Cola, the original, the real thing." Then the camera moved to reveal a can of Pepsi right next to the Coke bottle, and the voiceover implied that for some people, there is Pepsi, which has a sweeter taste than Coca-Cola. The two brands parted, and behind it was a can of New Coke. The next phrase provided the reason that New Coke existed. The voiceover said that there was now another option that had the real cola taste of Coca-Cola plus the sweetness of Pepsi. In other words, for those who liked the sweetness of Pepsi, Coke now offered a product designed just for them.

The communication did three things:

1. Reinforced the strength and leadership position of the mother brand (Coca-Cola Classic with the contour glass bottle and its famous Spencerian Script logo versus the can imagery of the other two).
2. Positioned Pepsi as sweeter than Coke.
3. Provided a new comparison factor. The comparable brands were now New Coke and Pepsi. New Coke was sweet like Pepsi, yet maintained the real cola taste of original Coke.

Coca-Cola still had to alleviate the third barrier (No one I know drinks it). To do so, Coke strategically adapted the classic spokesperson strategy, but did so to reflect regional values and attitudes, with the idea that localized associations could build stronger and more believable consumer relationships. In the test markets of Salt Lake City and Milwaukee, it used the most visible and credible local Utah Jazz and Green

Bay Packer players to showcase that there were people out there who were drinking and enjoying this new version of Coke. Of course, this was always done within the premise of clearly explaining what the brand was, why it was there, and who it was for. Packaging was changed to add a touch of Pepsi blue, in an unmistakable effort to attract competitive (Pepsi) users. To get consumers to "taste the brand again" and generate retrial, 16 oz cans were put out with the message "4 oz free!"

The campaign was launched in ten test markets and saw an average growth rate of 65 percent, almost all of it coming from the Pepsi franchise. Even the consumer imagery scores for New Coke, which had been abysmal prior to the repositioning, significantly improved. New Coke, a once blacklisted brand, was seeing resurgence in these local markets. Of course, this posed another strategic question: If the company decided to move forward with a national New Coke strategy, how could it effectively market two sugar colas?

Meanwhile, there was a growing trademark issue that needed to be addressed. As noted earlier, Coca-Cola Classic (original Coke) was technically the line extension, and "Coke" (New Coke) was technically the parent brand, albeit much smaller than the line extension. There needed to be a transition back to the Coca-Cola Classic formula's being the parent brand. This would require two things: a name change for the new Coke formulation, and a slow elimination of the word "classic" from the original formulation. A number of names were tested to replace New Coke, and Coke II was eventually selected. Hutcherson explains, "Coke II tested well and aligned well with the strategy. Coke II, like the ad said, would be for those Pepsi drinkers who sought out a Coke brand with Pepsi sweetness and real cola taste." The name would also reinforce the leadership position of Coca-Cola Classic and move the competitive taste claim battle against Pepsi to the number-two brand, effectively pulling the category leader, Coca-Cola Classic, out of the fray.

Hutcherson's old boss and mentor Paul Porwoll returned to the team to lead an even bigger marketing campaign to be tested under the new Coke II trademark, one fully capitalizing on the previous test-market learnings of "taste it, understand it, and see people like me with it." Hutcherson adds, "One of two things would happen. If it worked, it would set the stage for a possible large-scale assault on Pepsi to invite a large part of their drinker base over to Coke II, developing totally new and incremental relationships with their consumers. If it didn't work, it would have at least set the stage for the base brand to begin the reduction, and ultimately the elimination, of the 'classic' modifier and have the company be singularly focused on one sugared cola brand."

Declaration of War

Recall that in the late 1980s, the Cola Wars were in full bloom, and the two companies were in a constant battle for market share. Given the success of the New Coke test markets, the company was confident that Coke II could play a pivotal role in the market share competition against Pepsi. Nevertheless, The Coca-Cola Company still needed to test it to see what the implications would be for a national launch. A senior executive recommended that a test be done in Spokane, Washington. As Hutcherson says, "Even though we had done initial New Coke work there, it was a smaller market that we thought would be under the radar. We didn't even track that small of an area with our Nielsen market share and diagnostic tracking system." An aggressive Coke II marketing campaign was developed and then launched in the Spokane market in 1990.

Hutcherson explains, "We were going to go all-out to win over that young Pepsi drinker and ensure that the volume was incremental to and not take from Coca-Cola Classic. We ran the same type of phased communication message that had been so successful with New Coke and got even more aggressive with packaging innovation and price points. We did the 16 oz (4 oz free!) cans and then offered fifteen-packs at the same price point as twelve-pack cans on Coke II." The response was huge. In Spokane, Coke II immediately went from having a share of 0.5 to having a share of over 4 points, with research showing that it was disproportionately coming from the Pepsi franchise.

What Porwoll, Hutcherson, and the Coke II team hadn't realized was that Spokane was among the very highest per capita Pepsi markets in the entire country. In the context of the Cola Wars, Pepsi saw this as the equivalent of a premeditated attack on a heartland market, and it reacted in kind. Pepsi immediately produced a new advertisement showing three old guys on a porch showing the new Coke II graphics and saying, "They've gone and changed Coke again," a blatant attempt to confuse the situation and stir up old and unpleasant memories of the 1985 New Coke launch. Pepsi matched Coke II's sizes and price points, *across its entire brand lineup,* in one of its strongest markets. Pepsi's objective was to make Coca-Cola pay for doing this, even if it meant hurting its own profitability in the short term. Pepsi wouldn't just damage Coke II in eastern Washington; the company would try to damage the entire Coca-Cola brand portfolio. This was full-on war.

Back at Coke headquarters, a serious discussion was taking place as to whether this could continue. The brand team knew they had a winning proposition to engage in a relationship with Pepsi drinkers. But at what cost? If plans continued, many more markets would soon engage in the same war. Coke would spend heavily. Pepsi would spend heavily. If both companies put this many resources into fighting high-stakes battles within these small-to-midsize markets, their national marketing or R&D investments would most likely be significantly curtailed. Both companies might suffer significant consequences.

The other big question lay in how the overall market-share battle between Coca-Cola, Pepsi, and Coke II would play out. Hutcherson notes, "If Coke II was successful enough, you might find a scenario that looked like this: between the brands, Coca-Cola might have a 20 share of the soft drink market, and brand Pepsi might have a 17 share. But if the Coke share was divided as Coca-Cola Classic having a 16 share and Coke II having a 4 share, then Pepsi would be able to claim that it was the number-one cola brand. That couldn't happen either."

Finally Coke decided that continuing to try to use Coke II to romance Pepsi drinkers was not in its best interest and that it would end the aggressive and innovative marketing behind the brand and assign the resources to growing Coca-Cola Classic and Diet Coke. Coke II would be relegated to being a brand with little marketing support (beyond price promotions across the entire line) in a handful of strong Pepsi markets—to pick up what volume and incremental users it could. Ultimately, the company would stop producing Coke II a few years later.

Nevertheless, there were lessons learned. Hutcherson said, "At the end of the day, we were able to get a once despised and hated brand in New Coke/Coke II to be accepted again by a key strategic consumer group—and to actually sell." The team did what they needed to do to protect the trademark, set the stage for the original formula to return to being the parent brand, and manage New Coke/Coke II out of existence with little volume loss to Pepsi. There are times, for the greater good of the organization and the business, that a brand and consumer relationship must end.

ENDING THE RELATIONSHIP

It's tough to end a relationship. And all too often, companies aren't proactive enough in pulling the plug. Either the decision is made for them by a channel partner, or the brand just fades away with little fanfare. I can't ever recall seeing a "farewell tour" for a brand. Maybe that is something that needs to happen every once in a while. Management wonders what will happen to the volume and profit that was brought in by a dying brand. The few remaining loyal consumers have to find a new brand within the category. Maybe there needs to be a succession plan in place. All too often there isn't one.

Furthermore, what the New Coke story illustrates more than anything is something always to keep in mind:

positioning happens. Either you do it, a competitor does it for you, or consumers in the marketplace do it. In the case of New Coke, consumers spoke first. Coca-Cola only then succeeded when it aggressively tried to position Coke II as Pepsi's sweetness with real cola taste, to a very specific and valuable consumer group. For a brand that was presumed dead, it found a niche. It connected and started a belated relationship, one that was missing when it was launched.

Finally, we can use dead relationships as learning tools to further improve our existing relationships. From the New Coke scenario that played out some twenty years earlier, Coke was able to apply the learnings to the launch of Coke Zero. Instead of replacing Diet Coke, Coke Zero would meet a specific need. It didn't involve Pepsi, but it did involve providing real Coca-Cola taste without the calories.

One of my first managers on Powerade, Parra Vaughan, once told me, "If you don't make mistakes, you aren't pushing yourself hard enough." Marketers fail. Relationships disintegrate. It is part of the job. It is the natural cycle of existence. But if you do fail, fail forward. Fail in the name of the consumer. Fail for the betterment of the relationship. But whatever you do, don't keep things at status quo. Continue to give back to consumers and treat them with the admiration that you have for them.

• • •

We'll end where we began, with the definition of a relationship. A relationship is an association or connection. It comprises two parties who act for each other's mutual benefit. Always remember to keep your consumers' best interests in mind, and never stop learning about them and communicating with them. It is only by keeping the consumers first, by making them special, that brands live up to the definition of a relationship. It is the way we as marketers will show integrity in our profession, doing right by our brands and our consumers.

NOTES

Chapter 1

1. See, for example, Susan Fournier, "Consumers and Their Brands: Developing Relationship Theory in Consumer Research," *Journal of Consumer Research* 24 (March 1998): 343–372; Edith Smit, Fred Bronner, and Maarten Tolboom, "Brand Relationship Quality and Its Value for Personal Contact," *Journal of Business Research 60*, no. 6 (2007): 627–633; Atul Parvatiyar and Jagdish N. Sheth, "Customer Relationship Management: Emerging Practice, Process, and Discipline," *Journal of Economic and Social Research* 3, no. 2 (2001): 1–34; Barbara A. Carroll and Aaron C. Ahuvia, "Some Antecedents and Outcomes of Brand Love," *Marketing Letters* 17 (2006): 79–89.

2. Jennifer Aaker, "Dimensions of Brand Personality," *Journal of Marketing Research* 34 (August 1997): 347–356.

3. Fournier, "Consumers and Their Brands."

4. Ibid. See also Susan Fournier, "Exploring Brand-Person Relationships: Three Life Histories," product number 596093-PDF-ENG, Harvard Business School (Boston: Harvard Business Publishing, January 22, 1996).

5. Ibid.

6. See, for example, Fournier, "Consumers and Their Brands"; Smit, Bronner, and Tolboom, "Brand Relationship Quality and Its Value for Personal Contact"; Parvatiyar and Sheth, "Customer Relationship Management"; Carroll and Ahuvia, "Some Antecedents and Outcomes of Brand Love."

7. Steve Koonin, former VP of sports and presence properties at The Coca-Cola Company and now chief marketing officer at Turner Broadcasting, is a master at generating value from presence properties; he single-handedly changed The Coca-Cola Company's approach to in-event promotional marketing by focusing on having the brand be a part of the event rather than a static prop.

8. Martin Lindstrom, *Brandwashed: Tricks Companies Use to Manipulate Our Minds and Persuade Us to Buy* (New York: Crown Business, 2011).

9. Charles Duhigg, C. "How Companies Learn Your Secrets." *New York Times Magazine*, February 16, 2012, http://www.nytimes.com/2012/02/19/magazine/shopping-habits.html?pagewanted=all.

10. "Verizon's 'Precision Market Insights' Data Mining Policy Raising Privacy Concerns," *Huffington Post*, October 17, 2012, http://www.huffingtonpost.com/2012/10/17/verizon-precision-market-insights_n_1971265.html.

11. Quoted in Rosie Baker, "Unilever: 'Marketing Needs to Be Noble Again,'" *Marketing Week*, February 7, 2012, http://www.marketingweek.co.uk/unilever-marketing-needs-to-be-noble-again/3033850.article.

Chapter 2

1. Quoted in Dan Lyons, "10 Lessons from Steve Jobs That Every Marketer Must Learn," HubSpot blog, June 3, 2013, http://blog.hubspot.com/10-steve-jobs-marketing-lessons.

2. Christine Y. Chen, "Darius Bikoff vs. Coke and Pepsi: Business Is Flowing for the Godfather of 'Enhanced Waters,'" *CNNMoney*, February 3, 2003, http://money.cnn.com/magazines/fortune/fortune_archive/2003/02/03/336429/.

3. Even having kept the two brands separate, Nike sold the Cole Haan division in November 2012 to Apax for $570 million because

management decided it needed to focus on just its athletic brands. See Matt Townsend, "Nike Agrees to Sell Cole Haan to Apax for $570 million," *Bloomberg*, November 16, 2012, http://www.bloomberg.com/news/2012-11-16/nike-agrees-to-sell-cole-haan-to-apax-for-570-million.html.

4. Willem Jan van der Hoeven, global brand director, Heineken, interview with Tim Halloran, March 26, 2012.

5. All quotations of Katy Milmoe, integrated group account director, Havas Worldwide, are from an interview with Tim Halloran, February 26, 2012.

Chapter 3

1. All quotations of Kersten Rivas, managing director, Havas Worldwide, are from an interview with Tim Halloran, February 26, 2013.

2. All quotations of Katy Milmoe, integrated group account director, Havas Worldwide, are from an interview with Tim Halloran, February 26, 2013.

3. All quotations of Willem Jan van der Hoeven, global brand director, Heineken, are from an interview with Tim Halloran, March 26, 2013.

4. All quotations of Paul Smailes, global head of digital, Heineken, are from an interview with Tim Halloran, March 26, 2013.

5. *Sports Illustrated for Kids* regularly conducts informal, unpublished research among its subscribers for firms who advertise with the publication. The statement cited in the chapter is from research the magazine conducted in 1996 about kids' perceptions of sports.

6. All quotations of Matthew Kahn, chief marketing officer, Restorsea (former senior VP of marketing, glacéau) are from an interview with Tim Halloran, December 28, 2012.

7. All quotations of Scott Miller, president of Core Strategy Group, are from an interview with Tim Halloran, November 15, 2012.

8. "8 Beers Americans No Longer Drink," NBCNews.com, September 9, 2011, http://www.nbcnews.com/id/44460121/ns/business-us_business/t/beers-americans-no-longer-drink/#.Ug-rkKzB-So.

9. "Ad Age Advertising Century: Top 100 Campaigns," *Advertising Age*, March 29, 1999, http://adage.com/article/special-report-the-advertising -century/ad-age-advertising-century-top-100-advertising-campaigns /140150/.
10. Mike Celzic, "Michelle Obama Makes $148 Frock a Fashion Smash," Today.com, June 20, 2008, http://www.today.com/id/25280708/ns /today-today_style/t/michelle-obama-makes-frock-fashion-smash/#.Ug -ufKzB-So.
11. Share and sales growth data are sourced from syndicated services that measure marketplace sales data. For example, as of the fifty-two weeks ending April 15, 2012, IRI/Symphony showed smartwater as the top-selling premium water brand.

Chapter 4

1. Quoted in Stephanie Strom, "30 Years After Chia Pets, Seeds Hit Food Aisle," *New York Times*, November 23, 2012, http://www.nytimes .com/2012/11/24/business/chia-seeds-gain-popularity-for-nutritional -benefits.html?_r=0.
2. Joe Satran, "Chia Seeds Move Beyond Faddish Past in Bid for Mainstream Acceptance," *Huffington Post*, April 17, 2012, http://www .huffingtonpost.com/2012/04/16/chia-seeds_n_1419525.html.
3. All quotations of Janie Hoffman in the remainder of the chapter are from an interview with Tim Halloran, January 22, 2013.
4. Malcolm Gladwell, *Blink* (New York: Little, Brown, 2005).
5. "Janie Hoffman, Founder, Mamma Chia," BevNET, 2012, http://www .bevnet.com/bestof/2012/person-of-the-year.

Chapter 5

1. All quotations of Stuart Sheldon, president, Escalate, are from an interview with Tim Halloran, November 9, 2012.
2. Joan Schneider and Julie Hall, "Why Most Product Launches Fail," *Harvard Business Review*, April 2011, http://hbr.org/2011/04 /why-most-product-launches-fail/.

3. Theresa Howard, "Coke Finally Scores Another Winner," *USAToday*, October 28, 2007, http://usatoday30.usatoday.com/money/advertising /adtrack/2007-10-28-coke-zero_N.htm.

4. The sources for the discussion of the CZC and related data in this chapter are from the Stuart Sheldon interview and Coke Zero's 2009 WOMMY entry (provided by Sheldon), which won a Silver award for best strategic thinking to measure the impact/success of word of mouth.

5. Ed Keller, "Shining a Light on Dark and Super Dark Social," Keller Fay Blog: WOM Matters, November 7, 2012, http://www.kellerfay.com /insights/shining-a-light-on-dark-and-super-dark-social-ed-keller/.

6. Alexis Madrigal, "Dark Social: We Have the Whole History of the Web Wrong," *Atlantic*, October 12, 2012, http://www.theatlantic.com /technology/archive/2012/10/dark-social-we-have-the-whole-history-of -the-web-wrong/263523/.

7. Keller, "Shining a Light."

8. All quotations of John Doughney, client partner, Facebook, are from an interview with Tim Halloran, January 11, 2013.

Chapter 6

1. Christa Hoyland, "Chick-fil-A Ramps Up for Spicy Chicken Sandwich Launch," QSRweb.com, May 24, 2010, http://www.qsrweb .com/article/95197/Chick-fil-A-ramps-up-for-Spicy-Chicken-Sandwich -launch.

2. Tanya Lewis, "Chick-fil-A Finds Opportune Time to Unveil Spicy Chicken Sandwich," *PRWeek*, September 1, 2010, http://www.prweekus .com/chick-fil-a-finds-opportune-time-to-unveil-spicy-chicken -sandwich/article/177432/.

3. Ibid.

4. Chick-fil-A "2011 Fun Facts" http://www.chick-fil-a.com/Pressroom /Archive/fun_facts_2011_old.

5. All quotations of Jeff Gregor, chief marketing officer, Turner Networks, are from an interview with Tim Halloran, March 5, 2013.

6. TCM does show advertisements for its own products—promos for TCM movies as well as DVD collections for sale.

7. "Johnny Depp America's Favorite Actor, Harris Poll Reveals," *Huffington Post*, January 19, 2012, http://www.huffingtonpost.com/2012/01/19 /johnny-depp-americas-favorite-actor_n_1215685.html.

Chapter 7

1. All quotations of Jackie Jantos, creative director for global content, The Coca-Cola Company, are from an interview with Tim Halloran, February 25, 2013.

2. Jonathan Mildenhall, "Coca-Cola Content 2020," YouTube, August 2011; Part One, http://www.youtube.com/watch?v=LerdMmWjU_E; Part Two, http://www.youtube.com/watch?v=fiwIq-8GWA8.

3. Frederick Allen, *Secret Formula* (New York: HarperBusiness, 1994), 20.

4. Mildenhall, "Coca-Cola Content 2020."

5. All quotations of A. J. Brustein, senior brand manager, The Coca-Cola Company, are from an interview with Tim Halloran, February 25, 2013.

6. All quotations of Christy Amador, interactive marketing professional, Coca-Cola global interactive marketing, The Coca-Cola Company, are from an interview with Tim Halloran, February 25, 2013.

7. Mildenhall, *Coca-Cola Content 2020*.

8. "Domino's Says New Recipes, Frank Ad Campaign Help Double Profits," *USA TODAY*, March 2, 2010, http://usatoday30.usatoday.com /money/companies/earnings/2010-03-02-dominos_N.htm.

9. All quotations of Emmett Leopardi, the Leopardi Group, are from an interview with Tim Halloran, March 28, 2013.

10. All quotations of Jeffrey Cohen, VP and general manager, Meda Consumer Healthcare, are from an interview with Tim Halloran, February 19, 2013.

11. All quotations of Cigdem Topalli, senior brand manager, Meda Consumer Healthcare, are from an interview with Tim Halloran, February 19, 2013.

12. All quotations of Blake Hawley, marketing director, Meda Consumer Healthcare, are from an interview with Tim Halloran, February 19, 2013.

Chapter 8

1. All quotations of Jim Smith, senior VP of sales and marketing, Atlanta Falcons, are from an interview with Tim Halloran, March 6, 2013.
2. Phil Andrews, "Allen Iverson, Ray Emery, and Michael Vick: Three for the Money," *Bleacher Report*, January 6, 2010, http://bleacherreport.com /articles/320683-emery-iverson-vick-three-for-the-money.
3. See "NFL Team Valuations: #1 Dallas Cowboys," October 10, 2008, Forbes.com, http://www.forbes.com/lists/2008/30/sportsmoney_nfl08 _Dallas-Cowboys_300988.html. Note that as of 2013, the Cowboys were still the highest-valued franchise at $2.3 billion; "NFL Team Values 2013," Forbes.com, http://www.forbes.com/pictures/mlm45ekfed /1-dallas-cowboys-4/.
4. To view the "Rise Up" spot, see http://www.atlantafalcons.com/media -lounge/videos/Rise-Up—Featuring-Samuel-L-Jackson/2eb2a8ae-261e -11e0-9d26-00144fe56e6c.

Chapter 9

1. All quotations of Darryl Cobbin, president, Brand Positioning Doctors (former VP, Sprite business unit, The Coca-Cola Company), are from an interview with Tim Halloran, January 22, 2013.
2. Matthew Grimm, "Winning Ad Campaigns," *Advertising Age*, April 1, 2003, http://adage.com/article/american-demographics/winning-ad -campaigns/44764/.
3. Jeffrey Cohen, VP and general manager, Meda Consumer Healthcare, interview with Tim Halloran, February 19, 2013.
4. Malcolm Gladwell, *Blink* (New York: Little, Brown, 2005).
5. Ibid.
6. John Demott, "All Afizz over the New Coke," *Time*, June 24, 1985. Available at http://www.time.com/time/magazine/article/0,9171 ,959449,00.html.
7. New Coke/Coke II information and all quotations of Steve Hutcherson, partner, Trade NTE (former Coca-Cola executive holding numerous positions and roles, the latest being VP Coca-Cola brand business unit), are from an interview with Tim Halloran, March 21, 2013.

ACKNOWLEDGMENTS

I'm not sure when I actually caught the consumer marketing bug. It might have been when I was ten years old, and my father, who owned a department store in Titusville, Florida, let me not only join him on a trip to Atlanta to the annual gift mart but also persuade him to add an "NFL Shop" to the store (with decidedly mixed results). My desire to understand people's needs and meet them with the right product has only grown since then, cumulating with the book you hold in your hand.

Romancing the Brand would not have happened without a number of people who have shaped both my career and this book. I offer them my humble appreciation:

To Lawrence Lamont, professor emeritus at Washington and Lee University, who introduced me to the fascinating subject of marketing.

To my managers at The Coca-Cola Company who guided my development, teaching me that it is all about the consumer:

Larry Taman, who first hired me as a young assistant brand manager; Parra Vaughan; Ralph Kytan; Tom Reddin; Jim Taschetta; John Konradt; Frank Bifulco; Pina Sciarra; Steve Koonin; Jan Hall; Steve Hutcherson; Jeff Herbert; and Jim Chess.

To my Brand Illumination consulting clients, thank you for letting me get a glimpse behind the scenes of your intriguing brand and consumer relationships.

To Scott Miller, for all the guidance and advice you've given me over the years, a big thank you from one "General" to another.

To the students whom I've had the privilege to teach over the years, know that you've taught me as much as or more than I've taught you.

To all those who gave up their time to share their remarkable marketing stories, this book wouldn't have existed without you. Any errors that are in the text are mine and mine alone.

To all my partners at Jossey-Bass/Wiley: To Genoveva Llosa and Susan Williams, who believed in the concept behind this book enough to invest in a first-time author. To Clancy Drake, who was able to take the rough words I wrote and polish them into a coherent, logical manuscript. To Nina Kreiden for leading the entire production and copyediting process and to Michele Jones for your insightful changes in making this book read as strongly as it does. To John Maas for exuberantly overseeing the entire development process, keeping me on deadlines, having patience with me in wading through numerous cover options, and enabling me to provide input into the entire process—all with consummate professionalism.

To the marketing and publicity team at Jossey-Bass/ Wiley—Amy Packard, Michael Freeberg, and Ali De Leon— and to Mark Fortier and Norbert Beatty at Fortier Public Relations: thank you for your enthusiasm and energy in getting word out that we all, in fact, "romance the brand."

To agent extraordinaire Carol Franco of Kneerim & Williams, who came up with such a great title for this book: thank you so much for your belief in the concept, all the encouragement along the way, and all the fight you put in to make *Romancing the Brand* a reality. Here's to many more books in the future. Special thanks also to Jill Kneerim and the rest of the Kneerim & Williams team.

To my extended family: To my dad and first author in our family, thank you for your guidance, patience, and inspiration. To my mom, who taught me about showing kindness, love, and compassion to others, and backs it up as her life's pursuit. To my brother, Andrew, the second author in our family, thank you for your effort to show me the way through this crazy publishing minefield. Special thanks also to Billy, Lydia, Lina, Reyn, Mike, Double, Missy, Georgie, Brent, and all my nieces and nephews.

Finally, a heartfelt thank you to my family: my son, Henry, and twin daughters, Jane and Lydia, who are my three most precious blessings. To my wife, Dr. Nancy Hickam Halloran, thank you for the patience, encouragement, support, and love that you have given to me throughout this process and our life together. I am truly humbled to be your husband. "And that laugh that wrinkles your nose, it touches my foolish heart."

ABOUT THE AUTHOR

Tim Halloran has built and directed some of the world's largest brands. With over twenty years of brand management and new product development experience, he speaks extensively to business professionals on ways to improve the relationships between their brands and consumers.

Tim is president of Brand Illumination, based in Atlanta, and has provided guidance to top marketing companies, including Coca-Cola; Home Depot; Kraft Foods; Procter & Gamble; Delta Airlines; glacéau (vitaminwater and smartwater); Georgia Pacific (Consumer Package Group); Vita Coco; Sprout Organic Baby Food; the NBA; Intercontinental Hotels Group; Chico's/White House/Black Market; Atlanta's Fox Theatre; popchips; and Turner Broadcasting System, A Time Warner Company. Prior to consulting, Tim spent ten years in the Coca-Cola brand management organization, leading multiple beverage brands and marketing innovations. His successes at Coke include the national launch of Powerade sports drink and its sponsorship of the Olympics, codevelopment of Dasani bottled water, development of Coke's first Internet marketing initiative with his work on Cherry Coke, and the overhaul of Coca-Cola's U.S. tea strategy, including the creation of Gold Peak Tea. Tim has been featured as a brand expert in numerous radio, television, and newspaper outlets. He was awarded Innovator of the Year by Coca-Cola and named Max Award Finalist for Innovation by Georgia State University.

Tim has also served as an adjunct faculty member of marketing at both Emory University's Goizueta Business School and Mercer University's Stetson School of Business, where he teaches in the BBA, MBA, Evening MBA, and Executive MBA programs.

Tim lives in Atlanta with his wife and three children, where he enjoys coaching his kids' Little League baseball and softball teams and rooting on the Braves.

For more information, please visit timhalloran.com or romancingthebrandbook.com.

INDEX

benefits to, 65–67; repositioning New Coke by using spokesperson and visible, 222–223; TCM's "Cultural Engagers" and "Relevance Seekers," 135–136, 137. *See also* Brand evangelists; Consumers; Fan base

Innovation. *See* Brand innovations

Interbrand's *Best Global Brands Report*, 147

Interruption model of communication, 10

Intimacy. *See* Establishing intimacy

Intrinsics of brands, 10

"It's Possible" program (Coca-Cola Zero), 109

J

Jack Daniels, 71

Jackson, Michael, 217

Jackson, Samuel, 188–190

Jantos, Jackie, 147, 149, 153–154, 156

Jobs, Steve, 27

Jolly, Reginald, 205

Jordan, Michael, 79, 80

"Just Do It" campaign (Nike), 7–8

K

Kahn, Matt, 18, 62–63, 74–77

Kawakski, Guy, 27

Keep love alive stage: the Coca-Cola Happiness Machine event, 145–147; description of, 17; how innovation contributes to the, 157–171; "Where Would Happiness Strike Next?" campaign example of, 145–157

Keller, Ed, 113–114

Keller Fay Group, 105, 113

Kellogg Cereal City, 125

Know your type stage: description and process of, 16–17; developing a badge, 61–63; finding an association, 73–80; identifying your distinctive consumer, 55–57; laddering up benefits, 63–73*fig*; The Most Interesting Man in the World ads example of, 43–55; providing emotional and social benefits to connect, 57–61

Know yourself stage: description and process of, 16, 21–22; determine how you'll be different, 23–31; dig deep, 18, 23, 35–39; find the one thing, 23, 31–35; transitioning to emotionally driven connections, 39–41

Knowledge Networks, 138

Konradt, John, 207

Koonin, Steve, 208

L

Laddering up benefits: brand personality role in, 66–67, 69–71; brand pyramid illustrating, 71–72*fig*; creating smartwater's badge by, 63–67; essence of the brand illustrated by, 71–73*fig*; featuring functional and emotional benefits for, 64–65, 71; featuring social cachet benefits for, 65–67; increasing emotional connections by, 41; Miller Lite's successful approach to, 67–69

Smith, Jim, 19, 174, 177, 184, 189, 191
Social cachet benefits: "coolness" variable of product personality, 65–67; provide story value, 65
Social media: crafting the ideal experience through use of, 115–121; "digiWOMM" messages using, 112; innovative ways to use, 156; make it mutual role of, 113–115; "Open Happiness" campaign (The Coca-Cola Company) using, 150–152. *See also* Facebook; Technology
Southeastern Conference (SEC), 181
Sports: Atlanta vs. national top five, 180*t*; Powerade-branded equipment donations to school programs, 84–85; tapping into the emotional and social benefits, 57–61; understanding the mentality of, 57. *See also* Atlanta Falcons; NFL
Sports drink products: color as driver of purchase, 83; Gatorade, 24–25, 57, 79, 80, 85; teen consumer base of, 26–27. *See also* Powerade
Sports Illustrated, 174
Sprite brand: art of adaptation for repositioning, 210–215; building consumption frequency, 208–210; consumer market of, 197–200; coolness factor of, 203; five Cs of, 201–203; HCMs' perception of, 201–202; *Home Alone 2* message on, 199, 200;

"Image Is Nothing. Thirst Is Everything" messaging of the, 206, 209; "Lymon" taste of, 199, 200, 203; new focus on young males of color consumers, 200–201; new positioning strategy for, 203–205; selling the association of NBA and, 207–208; "Trust Your Instincts" advertising associated with hip-hop, 203–208, 209
St. John's University Coca-Cola Happiness Machine event, 145–147, 153–154
Stanford University, 8
Starbucks, 34
Starck, Philippe, 62
Stern, David, 208
Story value, 65
Storytelling: dynamic, 150; examining how The Coca-Cola Company excels at, 147–155; "Liquid and Linked" strategy of, 150
Sudekis, Jason, 51
Super Bowls: Atlanta Falcon's' 1998 play in, 176; Dallas Cowboys' five titles from, 183

T
TalkTrack, 112–113
Target: consumer data collection by, 13; Passion Index on fanship of, 142
Technology: emergence of marketing tools through new, 11–12; media stories on damaging results of using, 12–13. *See also* Social media